Assurance? Yes But Of What?

The Assurance Rainbow

A. Keith Anderson

Printed By
Remnant Publications

Cover art by Ellen Klim
©A. Keith Anderson

Assurance?
Yes—
But of What?

This edition published 1999

ISBN 0-9674634-0-8

FORWARD

The subject before us is a vast universe of sparkling luminescence, shared by the Creator with His creatures. Our challenge has been to select from this boundless pyrotechnic display a few sparklers from the mind of God that will fill a book of a couple of hundred pages more or less and ignite a fire within at least some of those who choose to read it. "Few will read *large* books," publishers say.

As I now view the task that was before me and compare it with what has been accomplished, I think I sense just a tiny part of the feelings of Sir Isaac Newton (1642-1727) in his later years. The comparison is rather incongruous because Professor Newton, who was also an accomplished theologian, is regarded by many experts in the field of science and mathematics as one of the three greatest mathematicians of all time (the other two being Karl Gauss of the eighteenth and nineteenth centuries, and Archimedes of the third century, B.C.). Newton's renowned work, *The Mathematical Principles of Natural Philosophy,* is widely regarded as the most influential scientific book ever written. In summing up the work of his lifetime, however, Newton had no boasts to make of his sweeping accomplishments:

> I seem to have been only like a boy playing on the seashore and diverting myself in now and then finding a smoother pebble or a prettier shell than ordinary, whilst the great ocean of truth lay all undiscovered before me.[1]

Prompted by Newton's metaphor of the "ocean of truth," I see many swimmers and surfers in the breakers along the

---

[1] *The Oxford Dictionary of Quotations,* Angela Partington, Ed. (4th edition; New York: Oxford University Press, 1992), 494, ¶ 7.

shoreline of the expansive sea of assurance that the inspired word of God, the all-encompassing testimonies of His Spirit, have provided us; but I look in vain for some finite bark drawing me out into the deep, to mysteries beyond the horizon that I have not yet seen.

I was dragged kicking and screaming by a most charming woman, Marcella, into this project after she, disappointed in what she was able to find *specifically* on assurance, or had heard from the pulpit or in seminars on this subject, felt motivated to attempt something in the area, and for months urged me to join her in the project. She had felt her heart warmed by what she had found in the inspired word, and wished me to join her in producing something on the subject for general consumption.

At first I was not at all interested, feeling somewhat like one of my four sisters who (to a reasonable approximation) exclaimed, when she found I was working in this area, "If I see one more thing on assurance, I think I shall go berserk!" She knew she was exaggerating, but her statement makes the point: I was certainly less than enthusiastic over Marcie's suggestion. Nevertheless I finally plunged at a venture into the subject and soon found my aversion diminishing, enthusiasm rising, and I rapidly moved up through the gearbox into high gear.

The result is that I have become quite ecstatic over what I have learned. The experience I have gained from plunging into this subject has been analogous to certain aspects of the following story told by a woman of a dream she had during a cholera epidemic a century and a half ago. My own experience assures me that the value of this story has not diminished with time.

> [In the dream] my husband proposed that we should walk
> out. In our walk I noticed that his eyes looked bloodshot,

4

his countenance flushed, and his lips pale. I told him I feared that he would be an easy subject for the cholera. Said he, "Walk on a little farther and I will show you a sure remedy for the cholera."

As we walked on we came to a bridge over a stream of water. He abruptly left me and plunged out of sight into the water. I was frightened. But he soon arose, holding in his hand a glass of sparkling water. He drank it, saying, "This water cures all manner of diseases." He plunged in again out of sight, brought up another glass of clear water, and as he held it up, repeated the same words.

I felt sad that he did not offer me some of the water. Said he, "There is a secret spring in the bottom of this river which cures all manner of diseases, and all who obtain it must plunge at a venture. No one can obtain it for another. Each must plunge for it himself." As he drank the glass of water, I looked at his countenance. His complexion was fair and natural. He seemed to possess health and vigor. — *Spiritual Gifts*, II, 113, 114.

And so to the reader I say, "Come on in, friend, the water is fine! 'Plunge at a venture.' It might prove a remedy for some of your maladies, as it has been for mine, and lift you to a level of assurance which you had perhaps not thought possible."

5

ACKNOWLEDGMENTS

I have been most fortunate to have had some very talented contributors, reviewers, and proof-readers who have carefully criticized the manuscript at various stages of development, and from a variety of perspectives. Their advice, guidance, sharp eyes, and encouragements are greatly appreciated. At the top of the list should go Marcella, my wife, who has great talent, and the rare quality of being happy to have that go unrecognized; and Elsa, our daughter, whose sharp eyes rarely miss so much as a missing period—and this while being a fast reader. Others who have shared their time and talent in a most helpful and constructive manner follow. With some exceptions, I have listed them somewhat in the order in which their contributions were received.

W. John Wilbur, Ph.D., M.D., and Bonnie—John is a research mathematician and physician at the National Institutes of Health, Bethesda, Maryland.

Richard D. Rockwell, Ph.D., and Joan—Richard was a colleague for many years in the Mathematics Department of Pacific Union College, and my department chairman.

John A. Scharffenberg, M.D., and Carmyn—World-wide travelers and health lecturers; John is my former teacher in symptom diagnosis.

Lloyd K. Rosenvold, M.D., and Leola—Gifted writers, and my former teacher in otolaryngology.

Ben and Pam Schreiner of Orinda, California—Ben has been with the Bank of America for many years in widely scattered parts of the world. Pam, a talented mother of four and Bible study group leader, has been especially helpful with Chapter

6

2; and along with Marcella, the Rosenvolds, and others, has kept pulling me back from the precipice of the indiscreet. They may not have entirely succeeded.

Maurice K. Butler, M.D., and Virginia—Lifetime self-supporting medical workers in the United States, Mexico and Africa, and enthusiastic healthful-lifestyle promoters. Among other things, the Butlers are responsible for the fact that much of the documentation has moved from the body of the text to the bottom of the page—an excellent idea.

Robert D. Wood, M.D., and Phyllis—If there is one person, a non-family member, who has had the most suggestions about the manuscript and grammatical corrections, it is Phyllis. She went over this with a fine-toothed comb, paragraph by paragraph!

Cover art by Ellen Klim, Santa Rosa, California.

The kind spirit manifested, and the correspondence, conversations, and telephone calls these contributors have directed to the author have all been most helpful and are greatly appreciated.

The structural mistakes and misconceptions that remain are the sole responsibility of the author.

INTRODUCTION

"Be careful [that is, unduly **anxious**] for nothing" [Philippians 4:6].... The disciple of Christ is not to bear a **troubled, anxious** countenance, as though he were **comfortless**. Said Christ, "I will not leave you **comfortless**" [John 14:18].[1]

The only thing for which each should have **anxiety** is to know how it is with his soul. The question to put to ourselves is, "Am I fighting the good fight of faith? Am I a living graft in the true Vine? Am I a branch of the parent stock, drawing sap and nourishment from Jesus?" How shall we know how to answer this question? Jesus has said, "By their fruits ye shall know them."[2]

At the very outset we observe that assurance may be considered under many different headings. We would like to look at it in this writing under two exhaustive, mutually exclusive categories—justified assurance, and unjustified assurance. David and Goliath provide excellent examples. In a certain sense, though in this writing they are not often mentioned by name, this entire book is undergirded by the confrontation between these two men. Both, in their fight to the death, felt highly assured of a favorable outcome, and in each case, for what would at first appear to be very good reasons.

David, a lean, muscular youth of perhaps 6 feet in height (plus or minus a little), probably weighed in the neighborhood of 170 pounds, more or less, but quite likely less than 200.[3] Goliath, probably a somewhat fleshy 9 1/2 feet (at least), perhaps weighed in the neighborhood of a half

---

[1] *Signs of the Times*, 11-30-1891, ¶ 7. Bracketed statement in the original.

[2] *Ibid.*, 4-18-1892, ¶ 7.

[3] We have estimated their weights from scriptural and other data.

8

ton, but very likely more than 900. In your living room with an eight-foot ceiling, his shoulders would be protruding through the ceiling into the ceiling joist space, and his head would be in one of the bedrooms of the second story. It would be only with considerable difficulty that he would be able to pass through the doors of most of our homes, and would make today's basket-ball professionals look like elfs. With these facts in mind it is most interesting and instructive that as they first faced each other on the field of combat, both felt fully assured of victory. The Bible story is found in 1 Samuel 17.

In the table on the following page are compared some of the parallels, differences, and reasons for these assurances of the outcome held by David and Goliath. With the above assumptions in mind it is not hard to understand why even "the armies of the living God," as David referred to them, were inclined to support the conclusions (except the last) of the right-hand side of the table. It is a remarkable thing that David felt so unthreatened by this tyrannosaurus-like monster. But that is the story of this book!—and the truth is that the world, in this current age of apprehensions, is not without its Davids. It is true, in fact, that *you* can be such an inexplicable hero (or heroine!) as David, the youthful leader of "those few sheep," who because of the supposed "naughtiness" of his heart had come to see the battle.[1]

---

[1] 1 Samuel 17:28.

THE FACE-OFF BETWEEN DAVID AND GOLIATH— JUSTIFIED VS UNJUSTIFIED ASSURANCE

DAVID—WEIGHING IN AT 170	GOLIATH— WEIGHING IN AT 1000
1. He had no doubts about who would win.	1. He had no doubts about who would win.
2. Because of number 1 he felt no fear.	2. Because of number 1 he felt no fear.
3. Because of numbers 1 and 2 his nerves were steady as he confronted the incredible hulk which was Goliath. His hand wasn't trembling as he reached into the pouch at his side for one of those five smooth stones—a calmness that was necessary if the stone was to be properly placed into his sling, and his aim true to the mark.	3. Because of numbers 1 and 2 his nerves were steady as he confronted this inexperienced, youthful midget (relatively speaking). His hand may have trembled a little from anger at feeling insulted, but not from fear. That anger would not interfere with the use of spear and sword as he had used them in many previous victories against much more formidable-appearing opponents. David appeared more like a bug to be stepped on, than a worthy challenger!
4. There was in his voice the ring of confident assurance, derived from his close relationship to God, as he accepted the challenge of the heathen monster.	4. There was in his voice the sound of self-confidence and pride in his hugely superior muscular strength, his armor, his weapons, and his skill in using them, as he disdainfully surveyed his pitifully under-equipped novice of a foe.

5. His trust was in "the living God" (1 Samuel 17:26, 36), the Source of his assurance. As he compared the power of his opponent with the power of his God, he was confident of victory in this (according to his thinking) obviously one-sided duel.	5. His trust was in his own incredible physical power and in the Philistine army at his back, the sources of his assurance. As he compared these with his opposition, he was confident of victory in this (according to his thinking) obviously one-sided duel.
6. For years he had been growing in faith and assurance in God's power and willingness to help him save his sheep with his staff and sling from powerful predators, and in composing Psalms and praising the living God with harp and voice. 1 Samuel 17:34–37.	6. Through a long history of successful combats against much more imposing opponents, he had been growing in such confidence and assurance in his own military prowess that he now felt David's challenge laughable and insulting. 1 Samuel 17:33, 44.
7. He felt assured that the power of the *invisible* forces—"the [real] armies of the living God" (1 Samuel 17:26)—who were ready to help him would be decisive. Similar reasoning and conclusions had previously served him well.	7. He felt assured that the prowess of the *visible* forces on his side would be decisive. He reasoned that, from the evidence, his opponent had no chance. Similar reasoning and conclusions had previously served him well.
8. The outcome of the fight would prove, beyond reasonable doubt, that David's method of evaluation was productive of right conclusions, and his assurance of victory justified.	8. The outcome of the fight would prove, beyond reasonable doubt, that Goliath's method of evaluation was productive of wrong conclusions, and his assurance of victory unjustified.

Part One of the book is a discussion of a growing list of thirty-six things of which anyone may be assured—a partial answer to the question, "Of *what* are we assured?" There is nothing magical about the number 36. It could be increased or pared down considerably, depending on the orientation of the author. Part Two seeks an answer to the question, *"Where* and *how* may such assurances be found?" As in Part One the answer, as must the answer to any such question, remains incomplete. Part Three presents some factors involved in assurance which do not fit nicely into either of the two previous categories.

For purposes of brevity this treatment of the subject is limited to a discussion of some of that inspired subject material which very specifically involves the popular term "assurance" and its derivatives and a few closely related words (such as confidence and certain forms of the verb, to know) as well as some of its antonyms (such as anxiety and fear), under appropriate limits.

With apologies to John 21:25, if this subject of assurance should be fully covered, "I suppose that even the world itself could not contain the books that should be written." The author wishes the reader a pleasant excursion into this important subject which gives such rewarding insights into the marvelous character of our heavenly Father and His Son Jesus Christ.

A WORD ABOUT SOURCES AND THE DOCUMENTATION

The reader will soon notice that most of the 600 or so footnoted references have no listed author. That is because most of these references are to the Bible (for which it is customary to give only book, chapter, and verse), or to one person, one of the most prolific writers of recent times, and probably the most productive of female writers of history— Ellen G. White (1827-1915). This woman, over a period of 70 years, wrote scores of books, large and small (currently published in many languages), thousands of periodical articles, and thousands more of unpublished manuscripts (many of which have been collected together and publicized via a variety of media since her death).

The prodigality of White's literary output is matched by the breadth of the areas covered. Hebrew-Christian history from creation to re-creation to come; practical godliness; counsels to parents, teachers and students; child care and family counseling; principles of dwelling house and institutional construction and location; concepts of healing and preventive medicine; evangelism; counsels to ministers and their parishioners; denominational organization and leadership; gardening and agriculture; and on and on.

I was first introduced to White's writings as a teenage soldier in the U.S. Army. The captivating interest which developed then continues to the present. My life, health, the ability to face crises calmly, the joy of living, and the ability to face the future with an eager anticipation for all it holds for me and others, have been profoundly influenced by these writings. Perhaps after you have finished reading this book you too will find your life has also taken on a meaning that is much richer, deeper, and more fulfilling and exciting.

I have tried to keep the documentation simple, and have not rigidly followed prescribed literary practice. My hope is that the reader may be able, with minimum effort, to locate sources and original contextual material. In particular, periodical sources are simply referenced by periodical title, date of publication, and in most cases, by paragraph number following the paragraph symbol, ¶. I have used a smaller typeface for the documentation and footnotes to make them as unobtrusive as possible, while still being readily available to the serious student. It should also be noted that upper case Roman numerals refer to volume number, whereas lower case Roman numerals refer to page numbers in the

Introduction to *The Great Controversy.* This Introduction was written by the book's author, an exception to the general rule that introductions are the work of editors.

The accuracy and content of all references and footnotes have been checked and re-checked by several persons, but humanity being such as it is, there may still be errors. Please bring any such to my attention, whether in the references, in the footnotes, or in the body of the text. You may thus be removing a stumbling-block from someone's path, and I will be most thankful.

A. Keith Anderson
751 Fairview Church Road
Spruce Pine, NC 28777-8223   Telephone 828-765-5644.

CONTENTS

PART ONE

ASSURANCE OF WHAT?

INTRODUCTION TO PART ONE

To some, perhaps many, assurance is an indefinable, abstract, comfortable feeling down inside that all is well—at times assisted by something similar to whistling in the dark past a cemetery. But assurance does not exist in a vacuum. If one has assurance he[1] must be assured of *something*—that he will be accepted into a chosen graduate school; that he can beat the odds at Las Vegas; that he will recover from an illness; that he can steal candy without getting caught; that God exists; that the world is 4.6 billion years old; that his sins have been pardoned; that it is right to destroy all the Christians in Damascus; that his spouse is faithful to him; that he can make the house payment; that there isn't the remotest possibility that the stripling, under-equipped David who has never faced a human being in combat, can overpower a half-ton, ten-feet-tall giant, trained in warfare, and armed with cutting-edge equipment, plus an armor-bearer.

As I search through the Scriptures, with the essential and always available guidance of the Holy Spirit, I find a broad spectrum of things of which God assures me. To provide a randomly-stated partial list: I am assured of acceptance, peace, love, pardon from sin, deliverance from sinning, freedom from fear, a new start (every day!), power (in spite of my weakness), victory, clear spiritual vision, a *personal* Saviour without and within, an eternal life of gladness, righteousness, uninterrupted communion with God, fulfilled promises, grace to provide for every need (spiritual, mental, physical), no more world-wide floods, God's hatred of sin and sinning while loving sinners, that Christ *has* come, that I

---

[1] In this book, as in the Bible, pronouns are often used generically. That is, "he" or "him" or "his" may just as well mean (under the right circumstances) "she" or "her" or "hers," respectively. Generally the meaning is clear from the context.

20

may become a child of God, that God and His word are true, that God hears prayer, that I may be filled with the Spirit, that I may be an effective witness, that Jesus is interested in what interests me, that neither I nor my dependent children will starve or die of thirst (but not that I will not be martyred or die of a lingering disease), that I (like Jesus) may be a partaker of the divine nature, and yes—when appropriate—of condemnation. You may have already noticed that the particular items between commas in this above list, to which you can likely add others, are highly interrelated. Like the colors of the rainbow, each blends into others. They are, in fact, all a consequence of one of the items in the list—God's incredible, unfailing love—and are made possible by the incarnation, life, death, resurrection, and present ministry of God the Father[1] and His Son Jesus Christ.

When one ponders such a remarkable rainbow as this, of assurances in the Scriptures, he begins to appreciate something of why the Scriptures *assure* us that we may have a rejoicing spirit—*in perpetuity!* But this spectrum of assurances invites more careful examination, to remove some of the human guesswork—and to add, as the occasion may warrant, some innocent speculation[2] of our own. As this examination proceeds, there will, I believe, be opportunity for there to enter our minds some understanding of why Jesus has guaranteed to us that our "joy may be full";[3] and why the Comforter has repeatedly assured us that Christians may be, and should be, "the happiest people in the world."[4] Since we wish to keep our focus on assurance, we will put that term, or its equivalent as may be the case, in bold-face type wherever

---

[1] If you find it novel to refer to the crucifixion of the Father, the following is offered in explanation: "God himself was crucified with Christ; for Christ was one with the Father" (*Signs of the Times,* 3-26-1894, ¶ 5); "In His Son, God Himself bore the penalty of transgression" (*Ibid.,* 11-4-1908, ¶ 13).

[2] "It may be innocent to speculate beyond what God's word has revealed, if our theories do not contradict facts found in the Scriptures." —*Patriarchs and Prophets,* 113.

[3] John 15:11.

[4] *Review and Herald,* 8-19-1884. ¶ 7. See also 6-10-1884, ¶ 12.

21

it occurs in an "it is written"—by someone with more authority than this book's author—context.

Chapter 1

ASSURANCE THAT GOD WILL ACCEPT US

One assurance must precede, and is an essential prerequisite to, every other—the assurance that Jesus, after His resurrection, received from His Father that His atonement was sufficient to provide full restoration (salvation) to the family of God for every rebel who would accept it; and more than this, that it was sufficient to assure the entire population of the universe that rebellion against God would never again arise.

1. CHRIST'S ASSURANCE THAT HIS ATONEMENT WAS ACCEPTED

When Jesus died for man, His Father's face hidden in the intense blackness surrounding the cross, He was plowing new ground. No one had ever before been asked to bear such suffering. One of His last living memories before his death was of His Father's frown of hatred for sin, and then nothing but impenetrable blackness from noon until three p.m. (as recorded in all three synoptic gospels). No other being, finite or Infinite, creature or Creator, had ever been called upon to endure such total isolation. This was the hell of all hells, an experience such as no other created being[1] ever would—or ever *could*—endure.[1] That He survived at all is a great mystery.

---

[1] The incarnation presents us with many seeming paradoxes, and some may question the propriety of referring to Jesus as a "created being." But thus does God Himself refer to Him—as both Creator and

Jesus died surrounded with such darkness that His senses could not penetrate beyond the tomb.[2] This was a new experience, even for Him. He was dying in the sinner's place, with no more assurance of ever seeing His Father's face again than the unrepentant sinner will have. He wondered whether sin was so offensive to God that He and the humanity He had humbled himself to adopt might be forever enshrouded in an eternal blackness.[3] Nevertheless He died not in despair, but in submission and faith.[4]

After His resurrection he refused to accept any homage until He had ascended to Heaven and heard from His Father's own lips the assurance that all that infinite love and wisdom had hoped to accomplish had been accomplished. Humanity was indeed redeemed. But more—the fallen race was to be exalted to a place with Christ on God's throne, to a place of participation in the innermost decision-making processes of the universe—a position the conquered Lucifer had dared to covet and which he sought to secure by force. The Son of *Man* was assured by His Father that He would carry His eternal humanity right into the highest, most private, and mysterious councils of the cosmos. A *creature* would be welcomed where no creature had been before. Thus that which Lucifer sought to obtain by force, Christ would

---

creature. For support of this concept see the quoted statement just below in the body of the text, from *The Bible Commentary,* VII, 926. Incredibly, the great eternally-existent Creator of all things became also—through the mystery of the incarnation—a created being!

[1] Cf. Isaiah 52:14; *The Desire of Ages,* 694 ("He had borne that which no [other] human being could ever bear; for He had tasted the sufferings of death for every man.") "Behold, and see, if there be any sorrow like unto my sorrow" (Lamentations 1:12).

[2] "The Saviour could not see through the portals of the tomb. Hope did not present to Him His coming forth from the grave a conqueror, or tell Him of the Father's acceptance of the sacrifice. He feared that sin was so offensive to God that their separation was to be eternal. Christ felt the anguish which the sinner will feel when mercy shall no longer plead for the guilty race. It was the sense of sin, bringing the Father's wrath upon Him as man's substitute, that made the cup He drank so bitter, and broke the heart of the Son of God." —*The Desire of Ages,* 753.

[3] "He feared that sin was so offensive to God that their separation was to be eternal." —*The Desire of Ages,* 753.

[4] "Amid the awful darkness, apparently forsaken of God, Christ had drained the last dregs in the cup of human woe.... And as in submission He committed Himself to God, the sense of the loss of His Father's favor was withdrawn. By faith, Christ was victor." —*The Desire of Ages,* 756.

accomplish for a created (human) being, not by force, but by submission and self-sacrifice.

God's law and name had been vindicated, and the universe forever secured from further rebellion—all without compulsion. It was the assurance, made to Christ by His divine Father, of all this that has made it possible for us who are made of the dust of the ground and of the breath of God to receive every assurance described in the word of God.

> Jesus refused to receive the homage of His people until He had the **assurance** that His sacrifice was accepted by the Father. He ascended to the heavenly courts, and from God Himself heard the **assurance** that His atonement for the sins of men had been ample, that through His blood all might gain eternal life.[1]

> In Christ were united the divine and the human—the Creator and the creature. The nature of God, whose law had been transgressed, and the nature of Adam, the transgressor, meet in Jesus—the Son of God, and the Son of man. And having with His own blood paid the price of redemption, having passed through man's experience, having in man's behalf met and conquered temptation, having, though Himself sinless, borne the shame and guilt and burden of sin, He becomes man's Advocate and Intercessor. What an **assurance** here to the tempted and struggling soul, what an **assurance** to the witnessing universe, that Christ will be a 'merciful and faithful high priest' [Hebrews 2:17]!"[2]

2. ASSURANCE OF OUR ACCEPTANCE WITH GOD

> Come now, and let us reason together, saith the Lord: though your sins be as scarlet, they shall be as white as snow; though they be red like crimson, they shall be as wool.... Come ... *all*.[3]

---

[1] *Ibid.,* 790.

[2] *The Bible Commentary,* VII. 926 (Ms 141, 1901).

[3] Isaiah 1:18; Matthew 11:28. Italic added.

The invitation to *come* is unconditional. If we wish to cast ourselves on the mercy of God, or to discuss our condition or circumstances with Him, we may "come now"—immediately—no matter how corrupt or seemingly hopeless that condition is, how heavy the burden has become, or how insurmountable those circumstances seem. Our condition could not possibly be worse than was the condition of Christ on Calvary, because He was bearing, not just the sins of one or of a few, or even of many, but the sins of the *whole world.* Though we are scarlet from head to foot with the worst imaginable sins, if we will come to discuss that fact with God, He will propose to make us as white as snow, as free of sin-burdens as the pure, wind-driven snow is free of blemishes. It is noteworthy that God compared the result with snow which is white through and through, and not with some object, such as a building that is white on the surface only. You can put snow into a grinder, and it comes out just as white as before. Stomped on, its whiteness remains unchanged. Put an object that is painted into the same grinder, and the superficial nature of its whiteness immediately becomes apparent. "Beware of false prophets," which are on the outside like sheep (white), but are in reality, more like "wolves" (dark).[1]

The important thing is that we need meet no conditions to *come* to God; while the door is open just come, like the rich, young ruler of Matthew 19, and tell Him the problem. He will always offer a valid solution which will, *with our permission and cooperation,*[2] be implemented despite how we may *feel* about it. The ruler came, and Jesus asked him to meet no conditions to be accepted into His *presence* and to

---

[1] Matthew 7:15.

[2] Here are conditions. It is important to notice that while there are no conditions we must meet before we may come to God and express to Him our problems, the solution God provides is not offered to us unconditionally—for example, our unconditional surrender to His rulership is required (see section 12 of Chapter 9).

be heard. However having heard his problem, Jesus stated a very case-specific solution that must be actualized by the ruler if his problem was to be solved, if he was to gain the rest and peace he desired, the assurance that comes from acceptance, not just into Jesus' presence, but into His *family*. He must experience a rebirth; he must, like Jesus instructed Nicodemus, be fathered by the Spirit, and be born into the family of God.

> You must not let anything rob your soul of peace, of restfulness, of the **assurance** that you are accepted [into God's family] just now. Appropriate every promise; all are yours *on condition of your complying with the Lord's prescribed terms....* [T]aking Christ's ways [solution] is the secret of perfect rest in His love.[1]

> We are to find the **assurance** of our acceptance with God in his written promise, not in a happy flight of feeling.[2]

> His dying love, manifested on Calvary, is the sinner's **assurance** of acceptance, peace, and love.[3]

> While in Arabia [Paul] did not communicate with the apostles; he sought God earnestly with all his heart, determining not to rest till he knew for a **certainty** that his repentance was accepted, and his great sin pardoned.[4]

Although we may come to God at any time, with any problem, we cannot come to Him with *full assurance of faith* until we have "a true [converted] heart,"[5] that is, are bearing fruit to His glory, fruit that is defined in Galatians 5:22, 23.

> How can we come to God with *full **assurance** of faith* if we bear no fruit that testifies to a change wrought in us by the grace of God, no fruit that shows that we are in fellowship

---

[1] *Manuscript Releases*, XXI, 230 (Let 130, 1898 to Elder and Sister S. N. Haskell; also partly in *My Life Today*, 176, and in slightly different form, in the *Review and Herald*, 4-25-1899, ¶ 7).

[2] *Signs of the Times*, 4-18-1895, ¶ 1.

[3] *Selected Messages*, I, 178f (1890).

[4] *The Spirit of Prophecy*, 318.9f.

[5] Hebrews 10:22.

with Christ?... What is the fruit that we should bear? The fruit of kindly words and deeds.... [Galatians 5:18-23 quoted.][1]

3. ASSURANCE THAT I AM A CHILD OF GOD

Whatsoever is *born of God* overcometh the world.[2]

The Spirit itself beareth witness with our spirit, that we are the children of God.[3]

The reason that so large a number of those who profess to be children of God always feel in **uncertainty**, is because they feel that they are orphans.[4]

This Parent-child relationship is not to be just a general one, such as *"we* (or he, she, you, or they) are children of God," although such an expression is often appropriate. The assurance here is of a very special, personal, and intimate relationship as if God and I were alone together, and I were His *only* child. This relationship is to be similar to the relationship between the Father and His Only-begotten Son. Redemption through the sacrifice of the *incarnate* Son of God has made me closer to God than even the pre-fall Adam and Eve.

A result of this intimate relationship to Jesus and His Father is that we will feel very close to each of God's other children—our brothers and sisters. Redemption so completely obliterates the past that we will feel perfectly at home in God's house in the New Jerusalem, at "boldly" entering without even knocking! And such boldness begins as soon as we "become the sons of God."[5]

---

[1] *EGW 1888 Materials,* 132 (Sunday, 10-21-1888).

[2] 1 John 5:4. Italic added.

[3] Romans 8:16.

[4] *Signs of the Times,* 11-12-1896, ¶ 10.

[5] John 1:12; Hebrews 4:16.

One of the reasons we are careful to knock before entering the home of even a dear friend here is because one can never be sure of what state of dress or undress in which he might find the occupants. As this was not a problem in pre-fall Eden so it will not be a problem in God's house—or, for that matter, in any other house in heaven, or anywhere in the new sinless universe. All will be clothed in the bright robes of light, Christ's righteousness. No one will need to remove these garments to "shower." In fact in a filth-free universe with no foul odors or offensive situations of any kind, it may be that there will be no occasion for "showering"; although we may delight ourselves in swimming in that mighty river of life flowing from God's throne—"waters to swim in"![1] We will find no locks on the doors. All will respect and give consideration to the individuality and privacy of others without these worldly barriers.

> The white robe of innocence was worn by our first parents.... A beautiful soft light, the light of God, enshrouded the holy pair.... But when sin entered ... the light ... departed.[2]

> For a covering, a beautiful light, the light of God, surrounded them. This clear and perfect light illuminated everything which they approached.... But when they ... sinned against God, the light of the garments of heavenly innocence departed from them. Deprived of the heavenly light, they could no longer discern the character of God in the works of His hand.[3]

We have yielded to the irresistible temptation to deviate somewhat into the future. Even now we may become members of the heavenly family, and have the assurance that we are the children of God.

---

[1] Ezekiel 47:5.

[2] *Christ's Object Lessons*, 310f.

[3] *Testimonies for the Church*, IX. 255f.

See that your life is hid with Christ in God [Colossians 3:3], and you will be filled with the most precious **assurance** that you are a child of Heaven.[1]

We want an arm to lean upon in the hours of affliction that can sustain. We want such an arm to rely upon when the earth shall reel to and fro, and be removed as a cottage [Isaiah 24:20]. We want to know then that God is our father, that our life is hid with Christ in God [Colossians 3:3]. Every one of you needs this **assurance**. The students at our school need this **assurance**.[2]

Not only is it our privilege to legitimately have the assurance *now* that we are the children of God; but through a disordered state of mind, it is possible to have an easy quietness about one's condition, a pseudo-assurance as it were, without the genuine realization that one is a true child of the heavenly family, the *redeemed* family of God, to whom Jesus is a very personal Saviour and Ruler:

It is *insanity* to be quiet and at ease as so many are at the present time, having no **assurance** that they are indeed sons and daughters of God.... [I]t is your privilege to say, 'I know that my Redeemer liveth' [Job 19:25]. The Spirit will bear witness with your spirit that you are indeed children of God [Romans 8:16].[3]

◆ For further discussion on the conditions of legitimate assurance that one is indeed a son or daughter of God see the sections "Assurance of a (Very) Personal Saviour" in Chapter 3, and "Assurance through a Redeemer-Ruler-Subject Relationship" in Chapter 9.

---

[1] *Review and Herald*, 8-14-1888, ¶ 9.

[2] *Signs of the Times*, 1-31-1878, ¶ 8 (Sermon at Battle Creek, 6-19-1877).

[3] *Review and Herald*, 11-9-1886, ¶ 14 Italic added.

4. ASSURANCE OF PEACE

> Peace I leave with you, my peace I give unto you.... Let not your heart be troubled, neither let it be afraid.[1]

> The Lord is my light and my salvation; whom shall I fear? the Lord is the strength of my life; of whom shall I be afraid?... Though an host should encamp against me, my heart shall not fear.... For in the time of trouble he shall hide me.[2]

One of the most basic and blessed components of the experience of one who has long been at war with God and who finally surrenders and makes Christ His Redeemer and Ruler, is the imperturbable peace that replaces conflict and anxiety. He may be in the very midst of tumultuous turmoil and panic, or captive of a merciless mob, but he is unruffled, in possession of unaffected composure and quietude. He is unafraid because he knows One who is all-powerful and all-knowing, and he is now that Person's friend and child. "We are ... his offspring." "Ye are my friends.... I have called you friends."[3] The Christian's Friend says, "Peace I leave with you, my peace I give unto you." "Let him take hold of my strength, that he may make peace with me; and he shall make peace with me." "Thou wilt keep him in perfect peace."[4]

> Ever learning of the divine Teacher, daily partaking of his nature, we cooperate with God in overcoming Satan's temptations. God works, and man works, that man may be one with Christ as Christ is one with God. Then we sit together with Christ in heavenly places [Ephesians 2:6]. The mind rests with peace and **assurance** in Jesus.[5]

---

[1] John 14:27.

[2] Psalm 27:1, 3, 5.

[3] Acts 17:28, John 15:14, 15.

[4] John 14:27; Isaiah 27:5; 26:3.

[5] *Review and Herald,* 4-24-1900, ¶ 7.

"The very essence of the gospel is restoration."[1] No matter what or how loathsome my mental, physical, or spiritual condition, God, the great Restorer, is pleased to accept me as a patient. He accepts me as I am, to restore me to mental, physical, and spiritual soundness. And I must accept Him as He is, to be restored by Him, as the great Physician Who knows what to do. He, the Physician, must be in charge—to give the instructions, and to perform what I cannot do for myself. This point must be fully settled in my mind before any progress can be made.

> Let this point be fully settled in every mind: If we accept Christ as a Redeemer [Restorer], we must accept Him as a Ruler.[2]

Once settled on this matter, that my case is in the care of One who has never lost a case that was placed in His hands, I have the peace that passes all understanding.

Calvary assures us that lasting peace can only be accomplished without compulsion, intimidation, or force of arms—that is, by love.

> His dying love, manifested on Calvary, is the sinner's **assurance** of ... peace.[3]

The sons and daughters of God are wonderfully assured of such love.

---

[1] *The Desire of Ages*, 824.

[2] *Faith and Works*, 16.

[3] *Selected Messages*, I, 178f.

Chapter 2
ASSURANCE OF LOVE AND HUGS

It requires but a brief inspection of the creatures God has created to be impressed with the design of the Creator that the desirability of closeness between living creatures is one of the principle features of the creation. Kittens and cats, puppies and dogs, baby birds, lambs, primates, whales, and a host of other creatures, the immature and adults, including human beings, and even insects (such as swarms of ladybird beetles), may be seen cuddled up together, or simply close, as they sleep, nurse, eat, travel, migrate, hibernate, &c.

5. ASSURANCE OF LOVE

God is love."[1] Is it any wonder, then, that perhaps the most wonderful, pleasurable, all-consuming experience that we can have is to be in love, truly in *love*—caught up in heaven's love, possessed by love, to be enfolded in His everlasting arms, to be forever inseparably close to Him! It is an experience that involves the entire being—body, soul, and spirit. It moves one to acts of unselfishness. It produces good, and nothing but good.[2] If you have had no experience with this phenomenon, it is your privilege to make a beginning in changing that state of deprivation *now*. The lived-happily-ever-after experience is

---

[1] 1 John 4:8, 16.

[2] "Pure love has special efficacy to do good, and can do nothing but good." —*Testimonies for the Church*, IV, 138.

33

attainable by all to whom "the love of Christ is preferred to the love of any [other] human being."[1]

We may have full assurance of God's incomparable love, and of our ability through grace to respond to it, to be delighted, thrilled, consumed by it, and to a considerable degree, imitate it. This divine-human experience then extends to inter-human experience. The possibility, importance, and necessity for us to "love one another" are frequently urged upon us in the Scriptures through several different writers: "As I have loved you ... love one another.... Ye ... are taught of God to love one another.... Love one another with a pure heart fervently."[2] Such love is possible only because God has such overpowering, unequaled love for us.

> [God] would have [His children] bear testimony to the fact that through the grace of Christ, they may ... find greatest joy in the **assurance** of his great love wherewith he has loved us.[3]

> [The Christian] will delight more in contemplation of the love of God than in anything earth can offer.[4]

> His dying love, manifested on Calvary, is the sinner's **assurance** of ... love.[5]

> Those who truly love God have **internal evidence** that they are beloved of God, that they have communion with Christ, that their hearts are warmed with fervent love toward him.[6]

Three times in Daniel, chapters 9 and 10, Daniel was told he was "greatly beloved" by God. This does not mean that God did not love Nebuchadnezzar, his

---

[1] *Review and Herald*, 2-14-1899, ¶ 3.

[2] John 13:34.... 1 Thessalonians 4:9.... 1 Peter 1:22.

[3] *Signs of the Times*, 4-11-1895, ¶ 5.

[4] *Ibid.*, 4-3-1893, ¶ 6 (This article begins on March 27).

[5] *Selected Messages*, I, 178f.

[6] *Review and Herald*, 5-12-1896, ¶ 7.

queen, Melzar, the Babylonian wise men, or Daniel's three companions, even though Daniel does not so record it. John 3:16 assures us that God loves even His enemies; but those who have passed from death in sin to life in Christ have a further witness within themselves assuring them that they have passed from being enemies of God to being His friends, and are personally loved by Him in a new, singular, and very special way. There is an atmosphere that surrounds us, a sphere of influence that can be detected by those within this sphere, and that has an influence upon them. "Love begets love, affection begets affection."[1] It is a glorious experience that can be distinctly sensed when one realizes that love for him is arising in someone else's heart and a heart-warming response is arising in his own. It is a hard heart indeed that does not respond in kind to genuine love.

> If you trust God, if you commit the keeping of your souls unto Him as unto a faithful Creator [1 Peter 4:19], you will have the sweet **assurance** of His love.[2]

Cleopas and his companion (who may have been his wife[3]) can tell us something about this inward, warming experience, this "fervent love" that burns in the hearts of those who walk with God: "Did not our heart burn within us, while he talked with us by the way, and while he opened to us the scriptures?"[4]

> Those who have a vital union with Christ will rejoice in the **assurance** of his love.[5]

Jesus loves *us*, as well as Cleopas and his fellow traveler. Love kindles a desire for closeness. Why then did He go away, and put Himself at such a distance from us? The

---

[1] *Testimonies for the Church,* II, 95; *The Desire of Ages,* 519.

[2] *The Upward Look,* 256.

[3] John 19:25; Luke 24:18.

[4] Luke 24:32.

[5] *Review and Herald,* 2-15-1887, ¶ 6.

answer is, So that He can be even closer! Closer not to just twelve, or to a crowd on a mountainside, but to you and me—everyone! Through the gift of the Spirit "He would be nearer to them than if He had not ascended."[1]

> It is a cause of rejoicing that we have an advocate with the Father, that our prayers ascend to the Father in his name, and that he is there to prepare mansions for those who love him, and also to prepare a people for those mansions. He gives us the **assurance** that it is because he loves us that he has gone away, because he can, by the side of his Father, better represent our cases.[2]

Although there are very strong feelings in such love, this love is not dependent upon something as fickle as feeling. It penetrates more deeply into the being.

> How can we possibly lead others to a full **assurance**, to simple, childlike faith in our heavenly Father, when we are measuring and judging our love to him by our feelings?... Let gratitude and thankfulness flow out of the heart, and cease to hurt the heart of Christ by doubting his love, which has been **assured** to us by most astounding evidences.[3]

> Herein is the love of God made manifest, "not that we loved God, but that he loved us, and sent his Son to be the propitiation for our sins" [1 John 4:10]. God has given **assurance** upon **assurance**, heaped gift upon gift, multiplied grace upon grace, and imparted his divine treasures to humanity, in order that we may believe the love that God hath for us.[4]

> Those who have a vital union [connection, closeness!] with Christ will rejoice in the **assurance** of his love.[5]

---

[1] *The Desire of Ages*, 669.

[2] *Signs of the Times*, 12-7-1891, ¶ 3.

[3] *Ibid.*, 12-3-1894, ¶ 7.

[4] *Ibid.*, 6-18-1896, ¶ 8.

[5] *Review and Herald*, 2-15-1887, ¶ 5.

6. ASSURANCE OF AN INTIMATELY PRESENT, ABIDING CHRIST

> I will pray [to] the Father, and he shall give you another Comforter, that he may abide with you for ever, even the Spirit of truth, whom the world cannot receive, because it seeth him not, neither knoweth him; but ye know him; for he dwelleth with you, and shall be in you. I will not leave you comfortless; I will come to you.... At that day ye shall know that I am in my father, and ye in me and I in you.[1]

> Abide in me, and I in you.[2]

> I in them, and thou in me, that they may be made perfect in one; and that the world may know that thou hast sent me, and hast loved them, as thou hast loved me.[3]

> God would make known ... this mystery ... which is Christ in you.[4]

Upon this subject the author of this book never tires of dwelling. These and other scriptures reveal that God desires to have a marvelously close, uninterrupted association with human beings, a closeness that was made possible only by the incarnation, death, and resurrection of the Son of God, and all that is attendant upon those accomplishments. Jesus, speaking of the Holy Spirit, His Representative, told His disciples that now, before the cross, "He dwelleth *with* you"; but that, after the resurrection, He "shall be *in* you."[5] The at-that-time current *with* relationship, even though it was quite close, was to be transcended by a future *in* relationship—"ye in me, and I in you."[6]

---

[1] John 14:16-18. 20.

[2] John 15:4.

[3] John 17:23.

[4] Colossians 1:27.

[5] John 14:17; italic added.

[6] John 14:20.

God has used the marriage relation to give us just a glimpse ("through a glass, darkly,"[1] as it were) of this intimate closeness, this "in-ness" union of God with a group of human beings called the "church," an experience for which there are only inadequate, defective parallels in the experience of *sinful* human beings. Nevertheless God uses such a parallel to cast a ray of light upon the marvelously satisfying and rewarding experience Christ's human associates are privileged to have with Him. With some trepidation we risk a brief consideration of such a parallel.

And why trepidation?—because Satan, realizing the beauty, power, and satisfying nature of the experience it is our privilege to have with God through Christ, has succeeded in all but destroying the beautiful parallel through which God has sought to illustrate something of the preciousness, the exalting transcendence, of the union He desires to have with us.

Note how closely Adam and Eve were bound up together. She was a part of himself:

> A part of man, bone of his bone, and flesh of his flesh [Genesis 2:22, 23], she was *his second self;* showing the close union and the affectionate attachment that should exist in this relation.[2]

Without each other the man and the woman were incomplete. The bride of Christ is to have a similar relationship to Him:

> Your work is to cooperate with Christ, that you may be complete in Him. In being united to Him by faith, believing and receiving Him, *you become a part of Himself.*[3]

> Ye are complete in [Christ].[1]

---

[1] 1 Corinthians 13:12.

[2] *Patriarchs and Prophets,* 46. Italic added.

[3] *Reflecting Christ,* 129 (Manuscript 44, 1897). Italic added.

In view of the above it is not surprising if when a man and a woman meet, an attraction should begin to develop. They desire to be together, to be with each other more and more. As affection grows, this *with* relationship becomes an insufficient means by which their growing affection for each other can be expressed. They desire to cast off reserve, to hold back nothing from each other, to share all they have and are. Before this can happen they must be able to *rest* in each other's love. The relationship must be secure from the intrusion of third parties, and other interfering influences. A mutually-binding, "everlasting" covenant is entered into, called marriage. Now, all fear of separation banished, the husband and wife are privileged to enter into that full surrender of each to the other which the Bible describes as becoming "one flesh."

> Therefore shall a man leave his father and his mother, and shall cleave unto his wife; and they shall become one flesh.[2]

The above scripture suggests that the marital union is not completed until *after* the man and woman become husband and wife—"they *shall* become one flesh" *after* she is "his wife." This is supported by the Spirit's warning to the Corinthian Church:

> What? know ye not that he which is joined to an harlot is *one* body? for two, saith he [Genesis 2:24], shall be one flesh.[3]

It seems clear that a man is unlikely to be of one mind, of one spirit, with a harlot, therefore becoming "one flesh" is convincingly a bodily, physical phenomenon—although one could certainly make a strong argument that the involvement of one's spirit is highly desirable. The point I wish to make

---

[1] Colossians 2:10.

[2] Genesis 2:24. Cf. Matthew 19:5.

[3] 1 Corinthians 6:16. Italic added.

is that God does not consider husband and wife to be fully united as one until the marriage is physically consummated in the full surrender of each to the other in the conjugal act. The apostle indicates that he is shocked that there are those who appear to be unaware of this fact. "What?!" he exclaims, at the thought of such ignorance. The story of Jacob's courtship of Rachel further attests to this. He served seven years for Rachel, but it seemed to him "but a few days, for the love he had to her." He did all this so that they might be more closely united. "Give me my wife," he said after the seven years of service, "that I may go in unto her."[1]

The Apostle, after pointing out the importance of Christians "preferring" others above themselves[2] in general, elaborates specifically upon the relationship between spouses:

> Wives submit yourselves unto your own husbands, *as unto the Lord.*... As the church is subject unto Christ, so let the wives be to their own husbands.... Husbands love your wives, even *as Christ also loved the church*, and gave himself for it.[3]

In pursuing this line of reasoning I have not wished to aggravate. But I may have nevertheless done so. It was mentioned, two pages preceding, that Satan has nearly destroyed the husband-wife relationship which God has used to illustrate the relationship between Himself and His bride, the church. In particular he has succeeded in reducing women in many cultures, even in Christian cultures, to little more than concubines—house servants and sex objects. Thus it is not surprising that many women, and some fair-minded men are offended by the scriptural counsel, quoted above, given to Christ's followers at Ephesus.

---

[1] Genesis 29:21, 23.

[2] Romans 12:10; Ephesians 5:21.

[3] Ephesians 5:22, 24, 25. Italic added.

Husbands, love your wives, *even as Christ loved the church.*" In the marriage between Christ and His bride, the strongest partner in the marriage—Christ—exercises no compulsion. It is left with the church to fulfill her obligations to Him, to respond to His eager knock at the door. The union of Christ with His church brings about a heaven on earth, and in heaven there is no compulsory obedience, but rather perfect freedom, the freedom granted by perfect love. And so it must be in the type; the physically stronger husband is to exercise no compulsion. The wife is not to be forced into submission, to be compelled to obey her husband. It is to be left with her to decide how she will respond to the soft knocking of his desires. The church, the Lamb's bride, does indeed have an even stronger obligation to respond to the wishes of Christ, her husband. And when she does submit, delightful indeed is the result. But Christ *feels no duty* to enforce upon her those obligations—and the consequent ecstatic happiness.

Similarly in the type, while the wife has an obligation to be submissive to her husband ("as unto the Lord"), the husband *has no duty* to compel this submission. Love, in fact, imposes upon him the obligation to renounce any such course. It is the failure to exercise this principle of love that has turned so many of our homes into miniature hells on earth, rather than a foretaste of the joys of heaven.

Continuing the metaphor of marriage provided in Paul's letter to the Ephesians, we see in Eden the result of turning this instruction around. Adam submitted to his wife in accepting her counsel to follow her in eating of the forbidden fruit, contrary to God's command. She became the agent in leading her husband to sin against God. He put his love relationship with her above his love relationship with his Creator.

41

For six thousand years God has been seeking to remedy the damage resulting from the effort of the bride, the church, to instruct her Husband, Christ, rather than surrendering to His wishes. This recovery process will be complete only when through the greatest demonstration of love that can ever be known Christ and His bride are brought into a oneness that will always be otherwise unequaled. Satan relentlessly opposes the accomplishment of Christ's cherished purpose, and he has been quite successful in enlisting the aid of many spouses. Is it any wonder, then, that men and women will leave no stone unturned to escape what are interpreted as the implications of the apostle's counsel to the Ephesians concerning the duties of husbands and wives to each other?

As in the context of the truly Christ-centered marriage, submission of the wife to the husband and the deep, considerate love of the husband for his wife, bring about the most endearing and enduring, exciting and ecstatic, loving and giving, breathtaking and transported, united and unselfish experiences *mortals* are capable of having; so the "marriage" (unification) of Christ with His church will produce the most overwhelming, grand, rapturous, prodigal, ravishing love experiences *immortal* created beings are able to have. As the married couple are ravished with each other's love, so Christ and His bride will be swallowed up in a never-before-experienced, rapturous relationship of Creator and creature. The delightful experiences deriving from the consummation of the union of man and woman in marriage, the unifying, ravishing experience that is the final step establishing them as "one flesh," exemplifies something of the overwhelming, breathtaking experiences that derive from the fulfilment of the previously-stated promise: "He ... shall be in you.... [Y]e in me and I in you."

This is indeed "Christ *in* you, the hope of glory." And that experience is designed to be as much more wonderful than the earthly union of man and woman, as the heavenly Husband is more wonderful than His earthly counterpart.

> Eye hath not seen, nor ear heard, neither have entered into the heart of man, the things which God hath prepared for them that love him.[1]

> The golden rule [Matthew 7:12] teaches, by implication, the same truth which is taught elsewhere in the Sermon on the Mount, that "with what measure ye mete, it shall be measured to you again." ... What we give does, in time of need, often come back to us in fourfold measure in the coin of the realm. But, besides this, all gifts are repaid, even in this life, in *the fuller inflowing of His love,* which is the sum of *all heaven's glory and its treasure.*[2]

One of the marvels of God's planning for the happiness of mortals is the manner by which the truly Christlike family is enlarged. It is in the ecstasy of the most intimate oneness, the marriage partners ravished by their love, that children are to be conceived. And it was as the result of the most intimate, breathtaking, exalting union with Christ at Pentecost that thousands were added to the family of God. Jesus "breathed on them ... the Holy Ghost."[3] What an expression of intimate love that was! Is it any marvel that Christ's enemies have worked so tirelessly to destroy the unity and stability of the family, and with it, the family of God, so that the family—and the church—may be enlarged only by giving birth to bastards! But, praise God, we need not so frustrate the grace of God. It is our privilege to be ravished by the intimacy of the Saviour's approaches, to surrender only to His advances, forsaking all competitors.

> As we study the plan of redemption, the heart will feel the throb of the Saviour's love, and will be *ravished* by the charms of His character. It is the love of Christ that makes

---

[1] 1 Corinthians 2:9.

[2] *The Mount of Blessing,* 136. Italic added.

[3] John 20:22.

our heaven.... [L]anguage fails us.... [W]e can but exclaim, "O the heights and depths of the love of Christ!" ... His love is like a vast ocean, without bottom or shore. In all true disciples this love, like sacred fire, burns on the altar of the heart.[1]

There are some ... who ought to be men instead of boys ... but ... the Saviour's great love has not *ravished* their souls.[2]

[M]y soul is *ravished* with the love which is expressed upon Calvary.[3]

[K]eep looking unto Jesus, and become *ravished* with the perfections of his character.[4]

From these assurances it should be apparent that the Christian's abiding love relationship with Christ is not a tame, apathetic, frigid experience. It is rather described as a transporting, "ravishing," fervent, delightful adventure, and is to be known for its ardor. We are still further assured of the possibility of such deep experiences.

It is not too late to **assure** ourselves that Christ is abiding in our heart[s] by faith.[5]

We must **know** that we are in Christ and Christ in us, or we cannot teach and lead others.[6]

Christ is formed within [the soul that loves Jesus], the hope of glory [Colossians 1:27]. His confidence increases that he is loved of God, and his love deepens and widens, as he has the **assurance** that he is abiding in Christ and Christ in him [John 15:4].[7]

---

[1] *Lift Him Up*, 248. Italic added.

[2] *Testimonies for the Church*, V, 263. Italic added.

[3] *Sermons and Talks*, I, 189. Italic added.

[4] *The Ellen G. White 1888 Materials*, 974. Italic added.

[5] *Review and Herald*, 8-27-1889, ¶ 1 (Chicago talk, 4-9-1889).

[6] Manuscript Releases, VII, 29 (5-20-1880).

[7] *The Youth's Instructor*, 8-9-1894, ¶ 7.

ASSURANCE OF WHAT?

We should feel a constant **assurance** that Jesus is *present.*[1]

It would not be surprising if by now in our discussion of the "ye in me and I in you" love relationship that is to exist between man and God and to some extent between Christian and Christian, the reader has become somewhat apprehensive and skeptical of what may be interpreted as a focus on feeling in all this, especially in the light of a considerable body of counsel warning us against undue emphasis on feeling, as contrasted with principle, in the Christian's experience. The key that keeps us on course is in the concept of *control* of behavior, often described in the Scriptures as temperance. Is my behavior controlled by Christ, by heaven-ordained principles and rules? If so, then my love is of God. Is my behavior controlled by my feelings, by *myself?* If the latter is true, then this so-called "love" may be nothing but a Satan-inspired infatuation, a preoccupation with self and self-gratification. If in the home each is preoccupied with the happiness of the others, God will breathe upon the inmates His Spirit and home will become "a little heaven to go to heaven in."[2]

> We are not to be controlled by impulse and feeling, but the principles of God's law must govern our lives.[3]

> The real greatness and nobility of the man is measured by the power of the feelings that he subdues, not by the power of the feelings that subdue him.[4]

> Whatever may be the ecstasies of religious feeling, Jesus cannot abide in the heart that disregards the divine law.[5]

---

[1] *Signs of the Times,* 3-31-1890. ¶ 4. Emphases added.

[2] *Review and Herald,* 4-21-1891. ¶ 4.

[3] *Ibid.,* 10-30-1888. ¶ 2 (Switzerland. 2-4-1885).

[4] *Testimonies for the Church,* IV, 656.

[5] *Messages to Young People,* 114 (*Review and Herald,* 11-15-1887).

◆ For further cautions concerning the place of feeling in assurance see the topic, "Assurance and Feeling," in Chapter 10.

The closeness, the intimacy of the relationship between Christ and His people is to be maximized in His *last* church on earth. The following revelation is in the context of the last-day, Laodicean Church:

> Behold, I stand at the door, and knock. If any man hear my voice, and open the door, I will come in to him, and will sup with him, and he with me.[1]

Solomon's Song provides insight into the love, the strong, affectionate desire, there is in Christ's knock, softly heard at the *bedroom* door of "the only object on earth on which He bestows His supreme regard."[2] In the following, the phrase in italic is from the Septuagint, a Greek version of the Old Testament in use in Christ's day:

> I sleep, but my heart waketh: it is the voice of my beloved that knocketh *at the door,* saying, Open to me, my sister, my love, my dove, my undefiled.[3]

The use of the word, "sister," in this verse, is in the sense of being a "sister in the faith," in the same family as the Bridegroom of the church, rather than in the sense of a genetic sibling in the flesh. Christ asks the bride He is pursuing to remove all the bars—closed doors—of resistance and reserve that keep them separated. What a delightful experience it is to a newly-wed husband when he discovers how completely unreserved and uninhibited is his new bride who before marriage, though quite affectionate, is surrounded with a certain atmosphere of unapproachable reserve.

---

[1] Revelation 3:20.

[2] *Testimonies to Ministers,* 15.

[3] Song of Solomon 5:2, *KJV* and *Septuagint.*

And what a delight it would be to Christ if His bride, the church, would remove all reserve and resistance to His advances and admit Him into the most private aspects of her being! Indeed, the expression "my dove, my undefiled,"[1] in connection with verse 6:10 and such commentary as found in *The Acts of the Apostles,* 91, ¶ 0, (and other places), is appropriately applied to the bride, the church—of the final days of this earth's history. This moving scene of Christ knocking at the bedroom door of "my love, my dove," is an effort of the Bridegroom to tell us that it is time for His bride—us, twenty-first-century moderns—and Himself to be on their honeymoon!

> Closer to Thee, my Father, draw me, I long for Thine
> embrace;
> Closer within Thine arms enfold me, I seek a resting place.
>
> Closer to Thee, my Saviour, draw me, nor let me leave Thee
> more;
> Fain would I feel Thine arms around me, and count my
> wanderings o'er.
>
> Closer, closer with the cords of love,
> Draw me, draw me to Thyself above.[2]

A serious question: Will the bride wait so long to remove all the barriers and reservations and welcome the Bridegroom in, that when she finally opens the door she finds Him gone?—the heart-breaking consequence presented by Solomon's Song 5:6. We wait anxiously for the answer. The wonderful prospect is that every human being is currently offered the extraordinary opportunity to right now make a start in entering into the closest, most sublime love experience that he or she has ever yet experienced. And this inter-human experience (with divine ramifications) will be

---

[1] Song of Solomon 5:2; 6:9.

[2] Mrs. E. W. Chapman, *Church Hymnal,* 1941 edition.

made as enjoyable and meaningful as a Human Being *Who is also God* can make it. The thought presents itself that when the Father, the Son, and the Holy Spirit created man, They did so because They wished to have beings with whom They could share an intimacy into which no other created being had entered. It is our privilege to be, not a frustration to God, but to cooperate in satisfying this longing of our Creator.

The love relationship between man and woman is to give us some understanding of our union with God, each responding to the approaches of the other in such a way as to maximize the delightfulness that the other finds in the closeness of this in-ness, this melding together into one of two persons—"abide in me, and I in you.... As the Father hath loved me, so have I loved you; continue ye in my love.... This is my commandment, That ye love one another, as I have loved you."[1]

Have you ever felt about some person that you would just like to hug him (or her) forever? This is the way God feels about us. Since Marcella and I first fell in love many years ago, I have often thought how nice it would be if the experience of holding her close could go on in a never-interrupted forever. In a small nearby church we attend there are a number of infants. One can see the mothers, fathers, and other friends of these little ones carrying them about with one arm beneath to hold them up and the other arm around to hold them close, and the infants enjoying every moment of it. It is such a relationship that God wishes to have with us: "Underneath are the *everlasting* arms."[2] He wishes to hold us close forever! And He hopes that we will hold Him close in a never-ending, uninterrupted, mutual embrace! *"Continue ye in my love."*

---

[1] John 14:4, 9, 12.

[2] Deuteronomy 33:27.

48

7. ASSURANCE OF CHRIST IN ME AND I IN HIM

This has already been discussed above under the preceding section of this chapter. We re-introduce one aspect of this subject here to re-emphasize its importance. We would not wish the reader to miss the glorious, uplifting assurance found in experiencing the indwelling Christ. Are you cast down? depressed? in need of rejuvenation, of an uplifting hand, of getting your life, your self-respect back? We need not be in doubt about how long is the reach of our Saviour, about how far down His hand is extended, about how close we may be drawn to God by the process and power of His saving, restoring love. Satan has some clever substitutes circulating out there, away from the heavenly influences, of which we need to beware. More may be found on these sly substitutes under the topic, "Unjustified Assurance," later in this chapter.

> Christ is our present, all-sufficient Saviour. In him all fulness dwells. It is the privilege of Christians to **know** that Christ is in them of a truth.[1]

> [H]ow shall we **know** that we are in Christ?—We may **know** it by the character of our fruit. The fruit borne on the Christian tree is holiness of heart—wholeness to Christ. God will be in the thoughts of the Christian, and he will love those for whom Christ has died. He will follow in the path of self-denial, and his life will be fragrant with the love of Jesus. *He will delight more in contemplation of the love of God than in anything earth can offer.* He will prefer his plain, homely duties rather than romantic novelties, and will be satisfied with the place God has appointed him.[2]

Although we now have some representation and assurance, in the closeness of the marriage relation, of what privileges will

---

[1] *Signs of the Times,* 9-2-1897. ¶ 14.

[2] *Ibid.,* 4-3-93. ¶ 6. Emphases added.

be ours in the never-ending future of oneness with God, our present view of the wonder of it all is seen with veiled vision. But the veil will soon be removed. And what if for some reason I have not yet married, or have very little prospect of ever marrying? Keep in mind that but few representative marriages ever happen, and that God is all-knowing, all-powerful, ever-present *Love.* It would be unlike such an all-sufficient Person to make no provision for such an everywhere-present problem. Indeed, He has a solution—Himself. The Bible asserts, "I [God] am married unto you"; "Thy Maker is thine husband."[1] "God shall supply *all* your need ... by Christ Jesus."[2] He is the faithful, ever-present, complete, *human* companion.

> "At that day ye shall know," without a dimming veil to obstruct your view, "that I am in my Father, and ye in me, and I in you" [John 14:20]. How many read this promise, so rich, so glorious, and yet *do not grasp its preciousness!*[3]

♦ The questions of companionless persons, spouseless parents, and others who have never married and what assurance they may have, are further touched upon in Chapter 8, Section 2.

---

[1] Jeremiah 3:14; Isaiah 54:5.

[2] Philippians 4:19.

[3] *Signs of the Times,* 11-23-1891, ¶ 8.

Chapter 3
ASSURANCE OF A GOD WHO LISTENS

8. ASSURANCE THAT GOD HEARS PRAYER

Amid the cacophony of confused voices and other sounds about us, we may wonder how anyone could hear our cry of distress; we may wonder whether our pleas are not caught away by the winds of evil sweeping around the world. But Someone is bending down to catch the most feeble cry for help. His ear can differentiate the entreaty of the needy soul from a million competing sounds created by the enemy to jam the spiritual energy waves. No word of praise or appeal for help, however muted, can escape that sympathetic, receptive ear.

> God will hear the prayer of the contrite heart; he says he will, and what better **assurance** can you desire than the word of God? Your weakness and sinfulness are all known to him.... Your very weakness may make manifest his grace and power; for your conscious weakness drives you to him who is willing and mighty to help when you lay hold upon him by prevailing prayer.[1]

> They that are abiding in Jesus have the **assurance** that God will hear them, because they love to do his will. They offer no formal, wordy prayer, but come to God in earnest, humble confidence, as a child to a tender father, and pour out the story of their grief and fears and sins, and in the name of Jesus present their wants; they depart from his

---

[1] *Review and Herald,* 5-27-1884, ¶ 3 (1883 General Conference).

presence rejoicing in the **assurance** of pardoning love and sustaining grace.[1]

There are three conditions given here that must be met if we are to have this assurance—(1) "prevailing prayer" of a (2) "contrite heart," and (3) "abiding in Jesus." God has given us gifts of His grace that make it possible for us to meet these conditions; and He has proposed self-administered tests by which we may determine whether these conditions are indeed met. (1) The condition of the "contrite heart"—true humility—is met if we are receiving "with thankful heart any provision made in our behalf, and with earnestness [doing] service for Christ.[2] (2) We may be assured that we are "abiding in Jesus" if we "love to do his will" (see the immediately preceding paragraph).

To some these conditions may seem hard, or impossible, to meet. But while it is true that it will be harder for some than others—especially for young people, perhaps—abundant grace has been provided so that these heaven-specified conditions may be met by all (we can never earn it or deserve it—if we could it would not be grace!). Fundamental among these enabling gifts of grace is the will, "the governing power in the nature of man—the power of decision, of choice. Everything depends on the right action of the will.[3] Grace has been deposited to man's account, but it must be drawn upon, put to use. To refuse to use it is to abuse it, and lose it. *All* is of grace, even our existence. It is in this sense that we—the whole world—are under grace. Further discussion on the omnipresence and sufficiency of grace may be found at the end of this chapter, under "Assurance of Grace."

---

[1] *Ibid.,* 9-11-1883, ¶ 16.

[2] *The Desire of Ages,* 646.

[3] *The Ministry of Healing,* 176.

It was suggested above that Satan has made it seem especially difficult for young people to lay hold of such grace. But to no one is it impossible:

> I appeal to the students of our schools and colleges, to believe in Jesus as your Saviour. Believe that he is ready to help you by his grace, when you come to him in sincerity. You must fight the good fight of faith. You must be wrestlers for the crown of life. Strive, for the grasp of Satan is upon you; and if you do not wrench yourselves from him, you will be palsied and ruined. The foe is on the right hand, and on the left, before you and behind you; and you must trample him under your feet. Strive, for there is a crown to be won. Strive, for if you win not the crown, you lose everything in this life and in the future life. Strive, but *let it be in the strength of your risen Saviour.*"[1]

Right here lies the root of much lack of assurance. We lack assurance because we do not realize how close the inspired word brings God to us. Our praying, our meditation, our investigation of the plan of salvation falls short of making Jesus a *personal* Saviour. We fail to realize that intimate relationship, that personal dialogue, that *mouth to mouth* resuscitation, in which God breathes into us His Spirit as He breathed into Adam in the beginning,[2] and which Jesus breathed into His disciples,[3] and which He desires to breathe into every sinner "dead in trespasses and sins."[4] Only as we experience this creative, redeeming work of God can we approach the throne of grace "with a true heart in full assurance of faith."[5] We repeat:

> They that are abiding in Jesus have the **assurance** that God will hear them, because they love to do his will. They offer

---

[1] *Review and Herald.* 8-21-1888. ¶ 17 (From a Battle Creek College talk at the end of the school year). Italic added.

[2] Genesis 2:7.

[3] John 20:22.

[4] Ephesians 2:1. 5: 5:14.

[5] Hebrews 10:22.

no formal, wordy prayer, but come to God in earnest, humble confidence;... they depart from his presence rejoicing in the **assurance** of pardoning love and sustaining grace.[1]

◆ More on the place of faith and feeling in prayer may be found under "Assurance and Prayer" in Chapter 10.

9. ASSURANCE OF UNINTERRUPTED COMMUNION

Lo, I am with you *alway,* even unto the end of the world.[2]

He is with us, not just collectively, but individually, and not just for an occasional grand, climactic rapture, but uninterruptedly. Friends, and even more so lovers, seek a place of privacy that their communion may not be interrupted. Small children resent interruptions in their parents' attention while they are communing with them. Contrariwise, we, individually, are privileged to always have God's full attention—as if there were not another person in the universe. God does not divide His "time" among competing interests. He gives all His "time" to each and every interest! This is difficult to understand because of our finite limitations. But the *omnipresent* God has no such limitations. He can be with me at the same time, and just as fully, as with someone on a planet orbiting some other sun in a distant galaxy. Time above has been enclosed in quotation marks because it is not possible to confine God by time as we understand time.

As long as you are true to yourself, no adverse power of earth or hell will be able to destroy your peace or interrupt your communion with God. If you fear God, you need not walk in **uncertainty**.[3]

---

[1] *Review and Herald,* 9-11-1883, ¶ 16.

[2] Matthew 28:20 Italic added.

[3] *This Day with God,* 334 (To Edson White).

We need quiet moments for meditation and prayer so that we will not be distracted from God. But God fortunately needs no such quiet moments to keep Him from being distracted from us, because instead of the finiteness of man's mind, He has an infinitely-many-track mind. He gives us His full attention while simultaneously carrying on all the infinitely many tasks to maintain the operation of an orderly universe. He loves us so much that He does not want anything to draw our attention from Him. "Pray without ceasing";[1] that is, do not allow anything to distract you from communion with God. This is a cure for the lack of assurance, the uncertainties, that so characterize the existence of those who can even momentarily be distracted in mind from Him Who is everything to us.

> We should go forth [to our work], not depending upon our talents, but wrestling with God for sanctification through the truth. We should feel a *constant* **assurance** that Jesus is *present* to help us.[2]

An immediate spin-off from this omnipresence of Jesus (through His Representative, the Holy Spirit and the angels under the Spirit's direction) is another benefit—we are never alone, which makes possible freedom from a whole host of problems that afflict the human race such as loneliness, depression, fear, and all of their multitudinous offspring. An essential component in all this is faith, because it is faith that provides the eyes through which we may see the ever-present Jesus "Who is invisible."[3] If we become forgetful of our closeness to God as His children, faith fails; and we feel like orphans. The result is a state of uncertainty and insecurity instead of the certainties of assurance.

---

[1] 1 Thessalonians 5:17.

[2] *Signs of the Times,* 3-31-1890, ¶ 7. Emphases added.

[3] Hebrews 11:27.

◆   In Chapter 10 there is further discussion on the relationship between assurance and faith.

The following statement has appeared before. It is especially appropriate here.

> The reason that so large a number of those who profess to be children of God always feel in **uncertainty**, is because they feel that they are orphans.[1]

We must overcome one-track mindedness. The man Christ Jesus is our example. In spite of the many distractive influences Satan brought to bear upon Him, His mind could be diverted neither from the task at hand nor from His Father above. This absence of a one-track mind is also possible for us, His genetic and spiritual siblings, for it is our privilege to "have the mind of Christ."[2] Like Him we may have our minds on the tasks at hand, and at the same time, God may be constantly in our thoughts. If we are tempted to respond, "But He also, as well as our human nature, had a divine nature," we may be comforted by the fact that, through the word of God, so may we partake of that higher nature.

> Through the knowledge of him ... are given unto us exceeding great and precious promises, that by these *ye might be partakers of the divine nature,* having escaped the corruption that is in the world through lust.[3]

This uninterrupted communion between the citizens and Ruler of Heaven assures us of armor and allies against all enemies so that, David-like and Daniel-like, the Christian walks through a world filled with Goliaths and roaring lions

---

[1] *Signs of the Times,* 11-12-1896, ¶ 8.
[2] 1 Corinthians 2:16.
[3] 2 Peter 1:3, 4. Italic added.

with a fearlessness[1] that is a mystery to men and to fallen angels.

> The life and words of Christ must be diligently studied, and his instructions cheerfully obeyed. He who will thus gird on the armor of righteousness need not fear the enemies of God. He may be **assured** of the presence and protection of the Captain of the Lord's host.[2]

We should not rest content until we, like the apostle Paul, have the assurance of continuous companionship with Jesus.

> While in Arabia [Paul] did not communicate with the apostles; he sought God earnestly with all his heart, determining not to rest till he knew for a certainty that his repentance was accepted, and his great sin pardoned. He would not give up the conflict until he had the **assurance** that Jesus would be with him in his coming ministry.[3]

The glorious prospect before us is that, unlike the men and women of the world, we are not limited to occasional experiences of transporting joy, but that "joy might *remain in*" us, that we may "rejoice *evermore*," even "in tribulations."[4]

> Nothing of the world can make [us] sad when Jesus makes [us] glad with His presence.[5]

And we need *never* be separated from that presence!

> [John 14:28, 12-14 quoted.] The faith here brought to view is not a casual faith; it is a living, earnest, active faith, that takes God at his word, and relies upon his pledged promises.... It is enough to make the soul joyful to have such **assurances**—a Comforter *always* with us, and we revealing to the world in hopefulness, in joyfulness, that we

---

[1] "Their only fear should be lest they surrender the truth." —*The Desire of Ages*, 356.

[2] *Signs of the Times*, 7-21-1881. ¶ 4.

[3] *The Spirit of Prophecy*, III. 318.

[4] John 15:11; 1 Thessalonians 5:16; Romans 5:3. Italic added.

[5] *The Desire of Ages*, 331.

have been called out of darkness into his marvelous light [1 Peter 2:9].[1]

10. ASSURANCE OF CHRIST'S INTEREST IN OUR INTERESTS

A major problem in families, in marriage partnerships, and in other groups, is that the individuals in the group wish to go off in different directions—in conversation, recreation, vacations, associations, living arrangements, &c. They do not share enough of the same interests. God assures us that He is interested in *everything* that interests us, collectively and individually. Although He may at times prefer that we go in a different direction, He will always ungrudgingly provide heavenly beings to accompany us. And as He accompanies us He will discreetly seek to lead us into such a relationship as Ruth had with her mother-in-law, Naomi:

> Ruth said, "Intreat me not to leave thee, or to return from following after thee; for whither thou goest, I will go; and where thou lodgest, I will lodge: thy people shall be my people, and thy God my God; where thou diest, will I die, and there will I be buried. The Lord do so to me, and more also, if ought but death part thee and me."[2]

> Let the souls who have been undecided and hesitating, trust in God, and no longer cherish doubt and unbelief; for they have the **assurance** that *Christ identifies his interest with ours.*[3]

At times God's angel sentinels may not be able to be as close as they might prefer, but they will never be far away. In a

---

[1] *Signs of the Times*, 12-7-1891, ¶ 1. Emphases added.

[2] Ruth 1:16, 17.

[3] *Signs of the Times*, 11-23-1891, ¶ 11. Emphases added.

world swarming with devils, "as long as there is hope" of salvation men are guarded by these heavenly beings.[1]

11. ASSURANCE THAT GOD KEEPS HIS PROMISES

Let us direct our attention, respectively, to two cases brought to the attention of Jesus—a devil possessed boy brought by his distraught father, and a leper.

> If thou *canst* do any thing, have compassion on us, and help us. Jesus said unto him, If *thou* canst believe, all things are possible to him that believeth.[2]

> There came a leper and worshipped him, saying, Lord, if thou *wilt*, thou *canst* make me clean. And Jesus put forth his hand, and touched him, saying, I *will;* be thou clean.[3]

There is an illuminating contrast between the way these two suppliants approached Jesus, and it may help us to come to God with greater assurance if we can understand this difference. In the first, the father questioned whether Jesus had either the power to prevail over the evil "spirit" that possessed his son; or, having the power, did He have the compassion to exercise it? In effect the father said, "If you *can* do anything, will you be *compassionate* enough to do it?"

In the second case there is no question in the leper's mind about whether Jesus *can* (has the power to) help him; his only question is whether Jesus *will* do what He *can* do—"If it is your will, you can exercise your power in my behalf to heal me." But that was what Jesus came to reveal—that a God of power *and* merciful love would help all who came seeking help, believing He *could* help—A God who could would. He came to correct the misunderstanding that His Father was a

---

[1] *Testimonies for the Church,* II, 222; VI, 366f.

[2] Mark 9:22f. Italic added.

[3] Matthew 8:2f. Italic added.

powerful, righteous, exacting God of justice with rather limited mercy. "The earth was dark through misapprehension of God." "To know God is to *love* Him." [1] The issue with the Jews and the world in general was not so much whether God had power, but whether He was disposed to exercise that power in a loving and merciful way. It was therefore the *loving* and *merciful* God that Jesus came primarily to make known.

Consequently we have a Bible that is brimming with assurances—promises—of help to the needy that recognize their need. The Bible is also replete with commands, that are really promises in disguise, that instruct us to do many difficult or seemingly impossible things—don't be afraid, always be happy, be Christlike, don't fret about where the next meal is coming from, be my witnesses (to all nations), stop sinning, sleep regularly, don't eat between meals, love God, love the unlovely (even your enemies), pray without ceasing, and on and on *ad infinitum,* until this page—and many more pages—could be full of dos and do-nots. The reason all these imperatives are promises is that every single one of them is an assurance of what God will do for and with us, that He will, with the command, provide the power, motive, and anything else that is needed so that the command may be executed, and human misery be reduced.

> [God] will not give commands without giving with them power for their performance.[2]

> I can do all things through Christ which strengtheneth me.[3]

> As the will of man cooperates with the will of God, it becomes omnipotent. Whatever is to be done at His

---

[1] *The Desire of Ages,* 22.

[2] *Testimonies for the Church,* II, 166.

[3] Philippians 4:13.

command, may be accomplished in His strength. *All His biddings are enablings.*[1]

And so it is that each of God's commands assures us that we are promised the privilege of partaking of God's powerful, omnipotent nature. That is why God's commands are among His most reassuring and motivating promises.

> God is the eternal, uncreated Fountain of all good. All who trust in him will find him to be this. To those who serve him, looking to him as their Heavenly Father, he gives the **assurance** that he will fulfill his promises. His joy will be in their hearts, and their joy will be full.[2]

> Why should not our joy be full—full, lacking nothing? We have an **assurance** that Jesus is our Saviour, and that we may draw freely from Him. We may partake freely of the rich provision that He has made for us in His Word. We may take Him at His word, believe on Him, and know that He will give us grace and power to do just as He bids us. He has given us every **assurance**, and He will fulfill all that He has promised.[3]

12. ASSURANCE OF GRACE

The entire world is under grace. "God has encircled the whole world with an atmosphere of grace as real as the air which circulates around the globe."[4] Apart from this atmosphere of undeserved divine favor[5] man would be ineligible for "a breath of air, a ray of sunshine, or a particle

---

[1] *Christ's Object Lessons*, 333. Italic added.

[2] *Review and Herald*, 5-5-1910. ¶ 9.

[3] *Sermons and Talks*, II. 293 (Sermon 3-10-1908).

[4] *Steps to Christ*, 68.

[5] A definition of grace, provided by inspiration, is "unmerited favor." See, for example, *Signs of the Times*, 2-13-93, ¶ 2; *God's Amazing Grace*, 182, 183. God has left no stone unturned, as it were, so that His adopted human family may walk through this dangerous world in the full freedom of fearless assurance. This is an incredible, and surely unmerited, favor. One could make a great case for, and write a book on, *unmerited assurance*.

of food."[1] The fact that we have air to breath and water to drink; and many of us have food to eat, houses to live in, beds to sleep in, and a monthly paycheck—that we even exist! is our assurance that "as there never was a time when God was not, so surely there never was a moment when it was not the delight of the eternal mind to manifest His grace to humanity."[2] It is in this sense that, in the mind of God, the new covenant—the covenant of grace—has always existed.

> By grace are ye saved through faith ... it is the gift of God.[3]

> Grow in grace.[4]

Grace is the measure of God's love and mercy. Satan argued that God could not, at the same time, be just and merciful, that justice and mercy are incompatible opposites, mutually exclusive; but he reckoned without love. God's love has given birth to twins—Mercy and Justice. And so, in a universe ruled by a God who is Love, far from being incompatible, mercy and justice are *inseparable*.[5] The divine

---

[1] *Faith and Works*, 21.

[2] *Signs of the Times*, 6-12-1901, ¶ 6.

[3] Ephesians 2:8.

[4] 2 Peter 3:18.

[5] "[L]et us always remember that Mercy is the twin sister of Justice." —*Manuscript Releases*, IX, 177 (1901). Mercy is not just the *sister* of Justice, but the *twin* sister. This stops short of calling them Siamese, or even identical, twins; but the fact that they are twins indicates convincingly that they are born together and that one cannot exist apart from the other. In a universe ruled by love, there can be neither justice without mercy nor mercy without justice; they have no separate existence. Calvary establishes such a relationship. Were the universe not governed by the concept of the cross (self-sacrificing love), such as Satan claims exists, Jesus might have cast off His mission of love, and returned to heaven, allowing men and angels to suffer without mercy the consequences of their rebellious sinning. God's creatures are incredibly fortunate that such is not the case! Love would not allow Christ to wipe the bloody sweat from His brow and leave man to the fate he deserves. Calvary and the scenes immediately preceding it (*The Desire of Ages*, Chapters 74 & 78) are the nearest a universe ruled by love will ever come to witnessing justice apart from mercy. The lost do not receive justice without mercy. Their final destruction, in fact, is an act of mercy *to save them from an eternally burning hell!* (Isaiah 33:14, 15; Hebrews 12:29; *Steps to Christ*, 18). Thus the full penalty for transgression of the law does not involve justice without mercy. Jesus, therefore, does not fall short of satisfying this penalty when He receives encouragement from a dying thief and the merciful ministrations of an angel when a God of love can "no longer endure the sight" of His suffering (*The Desire of Ages*, 760). The rhetorical question, "Did the Father spare his Son one jot of the penalty |"of transgression"|" (*Review and Herald*, 7-15-90, ¶ 6) does not imply that God can ever be merciless! The evidence suggests Love could never "endure" such a "sight."

nature defines every property of the universe. These properties exist only because God exists, and will continue to exist as long as God exists:

> [T]he glory shining in the face of Jesus is the glory of self-sacrificing love. In the light from Calvary it will be seen that the law of self-renouncing love is the law of life for earth and heaven.[1]

> Sin originated in self-seeking. Lucifer, the covering cherub, desired to be first in heaven.[2]

And so we have, in this usurped domain of Satan, competition to be first, might makes right, progression only through dying (of the weakest), survival of the fittest, and "the devil take the hindmost"—when actually he takes those who seek to be considered foremost. Grace was sent on its costly mission to restore this domain of selfishness to its original state of "self-renouncing love"—with the twins, Mercy and Justice, granted full citizenship, to which the scars born by the Saviour will forever testify—the scars of justice in the epitome of love and mercy. What a mystery! What grace! What assurance!

> By rebellion and apostasy man forfeited the favor of God.... He forfeited those privileges which God in His mercy presented him as a free gift.... This was the position of the human race after man divorced himself from God by transgression. Then he was no longer entitled to a breath of air, a ray of sunshine, or a particle of food. And the reason why man was not annihilated was because God so loved him that He made the gift of His dear Son that He should suffer the penalty of transgression [grace!].[3]

---

[1] *The Desire of Ages*, 20.
[2] *Ibid.* 21.
[3] *Faith and Words*, 21 (Ms 36, 1890).

You can say with David, "For all things come of Thee, and of Thine own have we given Thee" (1 Chronicles 29:14).[1]

These revealing words make it clear that every human being is under grace. We receive *"all* things," undeservedly, from God. This is grace—*"unmerited favor."*[2]

> I ask, How can I present this matter as it is? The Lord Jesus imparts all the powers, all the grace, all the penitence, all the inclination, all the pardon of sins, in presenting His righteousness for man to grasp by living faith—*which is also the gift of God.*[3]

God's grace assures our access to all these undeserved favors, all these blessings so necessary to continue our probationary existence, whether we are saved or lost. The difference between saved and lost persons is that the former recognizes the source of this grace and realizes how undeserved it is and how impossible it is to accomplish anything worthwhile for God without these sustaining graces. This is among the first perceptions of the newly re-born Christian. The apostle Paul provides a good illustration.

> While in Arabia [Paul, soon after his conversion] did not communicate with the apostles; he sought God earnestly with all his heart, determining not to rest till he knew for a certainty that his repentance was accepted, and his great sin pardoned. He would not give up the conflict until he had the **assurance** that Jesus would be with him in his coming ministry.... [A]nd he desired also to bear with him constantly the **assurance** of Christ's sustaining grace.[4]

The selfish person looks at his hardships and feels mistreated. He contends for his supposed "rights," and feels

---

[1] *Ibid.*

[2] *God's Amazing Grace,* 182f; *Selected Messages,* I, 331, 398. Italic added.

[3] *Faith and Works,* 24. Italic added.

[4] *The Spirit of Prophecy,* III, 318f.

he deserves better than he is getting. But when by grace he is converted he looks at the cross and the suffering Saviour and realizes that there is where he belongs and that anything better than this is undeserved. No matter what his state in this world he praises God for his blessings, even his "tribulations," which he now sees as blessings in disguise, and rejoices always.[1] The distorted vision of the lost sinner leads to all sorts of misconceptions. Error is seen as truth, and truth as error. Spiritual darkness is light, and light is darkness.[2]

> We cannot trust in ourselves; if we do, we shall fail.... We have the **assurance** that His grace is sufficient for us [2 Corinthians 12:9], and that we shall not be tempted above that we are able to bear [1 Corinthians 10:13].[3]

> I have listened to testimonies like this: "I have not the light that I desire; I have not the **assurance** of the favor [grace] of God." Such testimonies express only unbelief and darkness. Are you expecting that your merit will recommend you to the favor of God?[4]

> This morning one of the ministers remarked that he had been greatly helped in these meetings. He understood faith better than he ever had before; but he could not yet rejoice in the full **assurance** of the favor [grace] of God.[5]

No one need longer remain in such an unfulfilled state.

---

[1] Romans 5:3; Philippians 4:4.

[2] Matthew 6:23.

[3] *Signs of the Times*, 11-14-1906, ¶ 2.

[4] *Review and Herald*, 4-22-1884, ¶ 5 (1883 General Conference).

[5] *Ibid.*, 6-10-1884, ¶ 1 (Morning talk, 1883 General Conference).

Chapter 4
ASSURANCE OF A CREATIVE TRANSFORMATION

13. ASSURANCE OF DELIVERANCE FROM GUILT—PARDON

> Seek ye the Lord while he may be found, call ye upon him while he is near. Let the wicked forsake his way, and the unrighteous man his thoughts: and let him return unto the Lord, and he will have mercy upon him; and to our God, for he will abundantly pardon.[1]

The world and Satan have many ways that are claimed to relieve men and women of guilt-feelings, all based on tapping human resources, and all involving, in one way or another, self acceptance—accepting oneself as he is, and if there is any behavioral change at all, those changes need be only of such a character as to make possible acceptance by the peer group of unrenewed human society in which one wishes to function. Some of these methods produce spectacular momentary results, but the guilt "relieved" by such illusory methods will eventually "crush us."[2] Such a crushing weight of guilt can be estimated only at Calvary, as we listen to the anguished cry of our Saviour, "My God, my God, why hast thou forsaken me?"[3] as He bore the full weight of our guilt. That anguished cry provides human beings with some understanding of how terrible sin is, and at

---

[1] Isaiah 55:6, 7.

[2] *Thoughts from the Mount of Blessing,* 116.

[3] Matthew 27:46.

the same time gives us assurance that "no [other] man will ever have occasion" to himself give utterance to such a cry.[1] When pardoned, David rapturously exclaimed:

> Blessed is he whose transgression is forgiven, whose sin is covered. Blessed is the man unto whom the Lord imputeth not iniquity, and in whose spirit there is no guile.[2]

> David was pardoned of his transgression because he humbled his heart before God in repentance and contrition of soul, and believed that God's promise to forgive would be fulfilled. He confessed his sin, repented, and was reconverted. In the rapture of the **assurance** of forgiveness, he exclaimed, [Ps. 32:1, 2 quoted.]. The blessing comes because of pardon; pardon comes through faith that the sin, confessed and repented of, is borne by the great Sin Bearer.[3]

The conditions of pardon for willful sin (such as David's) have here been stated in some detail. David was pardoned "because" (1) "he humbled his heart ... in repentance and contrition," (2) he "believed ... God's promise to forgive," (3) "he confessed his sin," and (4) he "was reconverted." He had not rebelled against the prophet Nathan's stern rebuke. He had received "power"[4] to rejoin the family from which he, like the prodigal son,[5] had separated himself.[6]

> Confess your sins to Christ, and with true contrition of soul cooperate with him by putting these sins away. Believe that

---

[1] *Review and Herald*, 7-19-1892, ¶ 1.

[2] Psalm 32:1, 2.

[3] *Our High Calling*, 83 (Ms 21, 1891).

[4] John 1:12.

[5] Luke 15.

[6] This also shows that the "born again" (John 3:3, 5) phenomenon is a part of the process of justification (pardon). "[F]orgiveness has a broader meaning than many suppose. When God gives the promise that He 'will abundantly pardon' (Isaiah 55:7), He adds, as if the meaning of that promise exceeded all that we could comprehend (Isaiah 55:8, 9 quoted). God's forgiveness is not merely a judicial act by which He sets us free from condemnation. It is not only forgiveness *for* sin, but reclaiming *from* sin. It is the outflow of redeeming love that transforms the heart. David had the true conception of forgiveness when he prayed, 'Create in me a clean heart, O God; and renew a right spirit within me.' Psalm 51:10." —*Thoughts From the Mount of Blessing*, 114. Italic in the original..

they are pardoned.... Be **assured** that the Word of God will not fail.... It is as much your duty to believe that God will fulfill his word, and forgive you, as it is to confess your sins.[1]

◆ Further discussion of the relationship between faith and assurance may be found in Chapter 10 under "Assurance and Confidence (Faith)."

Encourage the sinner to go to Christ. If he repents of his sin, he will find abundant pardon. He has **assurance** that his sins will be remitted; for thus it is written.[2]

We appeal once more to a familiar statement used in Chapter 3 that overlaps, in a very important way the area being discussed here.

They that are abiding in Jesus have the **assurance** that God will hear them, because they love to do his will. They offer no formal, wordy prayer, but come to God in earnest, humble confidence, as a child to a tender father, and pour out the story of their grief and fears and sins, and in the name of Jesus present their wants; they depart from his presence rejoicing in the **assurance** of pardoning love and sustaining grace.[3]

The concept above that "it is as much your duty to believe that God will ... forgive you as it is to confess your sins" may create a problem for some. We can more readily see how we are to respond to a "duty ... to confess" than how we are to respond to a "duty to *believe* that God will ... forgive." This difficulty arises perhaps from our dealings with each other. If I wrong someone, it is my duty to go to them, confess the wrong, ask for forgiveness, and make restitution if applicable. It is not my duty to *believe* that I am forgiven. Indeed, I may *not* be forgiven. My duty ends with confession, asking forgiveness, and

---

[1] *Review and Herald,* 5-21-1908. ¶ 5.

[2] *Ibid.,* 6-13-1899. ¶ 13.

[3] *Ibid.,* 9-11-1883. ¶ 16.

making restitution, not in believing I am forgiven. The wronged person may react in several ways—a sweet spirit of forgiveness, the I-will-forgive-but-never-forget attitude, or outright rejection of any mercy whatsoever regardless of my attitude; and we are inclined to think God is like us.

And so how do I respond to the instruction that it is my duty to *believe* God forgives me when I confess, ask forgiveness, and make restitution if possible? There are two factors involved. (1) God *always* forgives if my repentance is sincere; and (2) He assures us that He will *give* us sincere repentance.[1] By faith in His word, I can therefore ask for repentance and believe that I am forgiven. By faith I can ask for anything I need (including repentance and forgiveness), and believe that I have them. It is not complicated, but it may require some earnest wrestling with God in prayer. The apostle Paul's experience in Arabia may again shed some light here.

> While in Arabia ... he sought God earnestly with all his heart, determining not to rest[2] till he knew for a **certainty** that his repentance was accepted, and his great sin pardoned.[3]

We are not asked to go to Arabia, or to conjure up on our own a belief that does not exist; but we may need to withdraw to the closet or to the upper room for a longer, closer visit with God than has heretofore been our habit. We can be assured that God "will not give commands without giving with them power for their performance."[4] It is our privilege to come to God and to take hold of Him with the

---

[1] 1 John 1:9; Acts 5:31.

[2] This does not necessarily imply that he did not sleep, but that he continued the struggle until he had received assurance that he was forgiven. In the opinion of the author of this book this is similar to a person's not resting from—giving up—a task, such as building a house, until it is completed.

[3] *Spirit of Prophecy*, III, 318f.

[4] *Testimonies for the Church*, II, 166.

resolve of Jacob[1] that we will not let Him go until we have the assurance of His blessing.

> Let us therefore come boldly unto the throne of grace, that we may obtain mercy, and find grace to help in time of need.[2]

14. ASSURANCE OF CONVERSION (NEW BIRTH, RE-CREATION)

> Except a man be born of water and of the Spirit, he cannot enter into the kingdom of God.[3]

> If any man be in Christ, he is a new creature [a new creation]: old things are passed away; behold, all things are become new.[4]

> Know ye not, that so many of us as were baptized into Jesus Christ were baptized into his death? Therefore we are buried with him by baptism unto death: that like as Christ was raised up from the dead by the glory of the Father, even so we also should walk in newness of life.... Knowing this, that our old man is crucified with him, that the body of sin might be destroyed, that henceforth we should not serve sin. For he that is dead is freed from sin.[5]

> And you hath he quickened, who were dead in trespasses and sins.... God, who is rich in mercy, for his great love wherewith he loved us, Even when we were dead in sins, hath quickened us together with Christ.[6]

> Wherefore it saith, Awake thou that sleepest, and arise from the dead, and Christ shall give thee light.[7]

---

[1] Genesis 32:26.

[2] Hebrews 4:16.

[3] John 3:5.

[4] 2 Corinthians 5:17.

[5] Romans 6:3, 4, 6, 7.

[6] Ephesians 2:1, 4, 5.

[7] Ephesians 5:14 (margin).

Since the above writings assert that conversion (the "new birth," experiencing a "new creation," death of the "old man" with accompanying "newness of life") is essential to salvation, it would be surprising, God being the kind of Person He is, if there were no means by which one could be assured that he has met this condition. When a person surrenders himself to Christ, to the working of the Holy Spirit, a new creature emerges from the hand of God with different likes, dislikes, and interests. The same stimulus now produces a much different response. Much which was dull and uninteresting, such as the Word of God, becomes absorbing and magnetically attractive. Many things that once attracted him, such as the lustful or violent, now repel. Much of what was appealing to his senses has become offensive. There is a sense of being washed in the blood of Christ, of being clothed in His righteousness, and that one is loved and valued by Him, is precious in His sight.

> The thoughtless and wayward become serious. The hardened repent of their sins, and the faithless believe. The gambler, the drunkard, the licentious, become steady, sober, and pure. The rebellious and obstinate become meek and Christlike. When we see these changes in the character, we may be **assured** that the converting power of God has transformed the entire man. We saw not the Holy Spirit, but we saw the evidence of its work on the changed character [John 3:8].[1]

> [T]hough young in the faith, you may **know** that you have passed from death unto life, if the fruits of the Spirit [Galatians 5:22, 23] are made manifest in your life. If you are growing in faith and hope and love, you may **know** that your spiritual vision has been cleared. If you delight to dwell upon the plan of salvation, upon the glorious manifestations of the divine character, if your heart, in contemplation of the love of God, glows with thankfulness and joy, you may be **sure** that you have been illuminated by

[1] *Review and Herald*, 5-5-1896, ¶ 3.

the beams of the Holy Spirit, and heavenly agencies are bringing your character up to maturity of Christian life.[1]

The believer commits his soul and body to God, and with **assurance** may say, Christ is able to keep that which I have committed unto Him against that day [2 Timothy 1:12].... There will be an **assurance** that the soul is washed in the blood of Christ and clothed with His righteousness and precious in the sight of Jesus.[2]

♦ See also the topic below, "Assurance of a (Very) Personal Saviour."

15. ASSURANCE OF DELIVERANCE FROM SINNING

The Word of God abounds with guarantees—"promises"— that, through the gift of the righteousness of the sinless Saviour, man may gain complete victory over sinning. Our concern in this book is with an internal *experience* in "assurance" that goes beyond the oftentimes rather austere function of an external warranty. This experience, though internal, is not internally *generated*, and should therefore not be confused with existentialism. And although often productive of very strong feelings, it should not be confused with mere "emotions" (see elsewhere in this book under the topics "Assurance and Feeling" and "Assurance and Faith").

It was Christ who from the bush on Mount Horeb spoke to Moses saying, "I AM THAT I AM.... I AM hath sent me unto you." Exodus 3:14. This was the pledge of Israel's deliverance [from the Egyptians]. So when He came "in the likeness of men" [Philippians 2:7], He declared Himself the I AM.... "I AM the Good Shepherd." "I AM the living Bread." "I AM the Way, the Truth, and the Life." [John 10:11; 6:51; 14:6] ... I AM the **assurance** of every promise. I AM; be not afraid. "God with us" [Matthew

---

[1] *Signs of the Times*, 3-27-1893, ¶ 6.
[2] *EGW 1888 Materials*, II, 495 (11-4-1889).

1:23] is the **surety** of our deliverance from sin, the **assurance** of our power to obey the law of heaven.[1]

A "surety" is "something that gives assurance"—Webster. It is, therefore, "God with us," the "I AM," (His ubiquitous presence, His timelessness—or *timeliness*) that provides those assurances that are being discussed in this book. Further discussion may be found in Chapter 2 under the topic, "Assurance of an Intimately Present, Abiding Christ."

16. ASSURANCE OF RECEIVING THE HOLY SPIRIT

If ye ... know how to give good gifts unto your children, How much more shall your heavenly Father give the Holy Spirit to them that ask him.... [T]he Father ... shall give you another Comforter.... [T]he Comforter, which is the Holy Ghost ... shall teach you all things.... I have yet many things to say unto you, but ye cannot bear them now. Howbeit when he, the Spirit of truth is come, he will guide you into all truth.... [B]e filled with the Spirit.[2]

Have not the precious words spoken by Christ, the Prince of God, an **assurance** and power that should have great influence upon us, that our heavenly Father is more willing to give the Holy Spirit to them that ask Him than parents are to give good gifts to their children? [Luke 11:13].[3]

This splendid gift of the Holy Spirit is freely offered. Why, then, do so few have the "assurance and power" that accompany this gift? It is because we are glad to have the "assurance and power," but are unwilling to be *guided and controlled* by the Source of this experience. Human ingenuity has been taxed to the utmost to evade the Spirit's guidance and control. Whole books have been written, accusing this heavenly Being of lying! And this is the case specifically because He has told the truth! Jesus said

---

[1] *The Desire of Ages*, 24f. Capitalized words in original.

[2] Luke 11:13; John 14:16, 26; 16:12, 13; Ephesians 5:18.

[3] *Selected Message*, II, 243 (Letter 7, 1892).

to those who were haggling over whether His interpretations of the scriptures were correct, "Because I tell you the truth, ye believe me not."[1]

The implication that they needed to be corrected by His teachings could, had they permitted it, have had a restorative influence upon them; but instead it irritated them and they allowed Satan to fill them with hostility. The last church of history—Laodicea—repeats this unfortunate experience of the church of Christ's day. It refuses to receive the "correction" Christ brings through His Representative, the Holy Spirit.[2] And so there is in this last church little assurance, little freedom from the fears and insecurities that characterize the world. Laodicea is whistling through the dark, specter-filled graveyards of this world—man-made assurance, human talking and planning, guiding and controlling. Déjà vu (Revelation 3:17)!

> There are many who believe and profess to claim the Lord's promise; they talk *about* Christ and *about* the Holy Spirit, yet receive no benefit. They do not surrender the soul to be guided and controlled by the divine agencies. We cannot use the Holy Spirit. The Spirit is to use us. Through the Spirit God works in His people "to will and to do of His good pleasure." Philippians 2:13. But many will not submit to this. They want to manage themselves. This is why they do not receive the heavenly gift. Only to those who wait humbly upon God, who watch for His guidance and grace, is the Spirit given. The power of God awaits their demand and reception. This promised blessing, claimed by faith, brings all other blessings in its train.[3]

This challenging, informative counsel implies that a comprehensive investigation of the assurances provided by

---

[1] John 8:45.

[2] "[T]he greatest reason why the people of God are now found in this state of [Laodicean] spiritual blindness, is that *they will not receive correction*." —*Testimonies for the Church*, III, 254, 255. Italic added.

[3] *The Desire of Ages*, 672. Italic in the original. Underscoring added.

the Holy Spirit would render repetitious the many approaches to this subject in this book. However, since God—unwilling "that any should perish"[1]—has chosen to repeat Himself in such a multitude of ways, we have followed His leading and have viewed "assurance" from many different perspectives. But here in this brief section we offer just a molecule or so of those specific situations where we are *literally and specifically assured* that we may, if we choose, be filled, guided, and controlled by the Holy Spirit, and that we may, with great power, be a means by which this divine Spirit and His many gifts are shared with others, providing them with the means of walking through this fearful world without fear.

> We shall be entrusted with the Holy Spirit according to our capacity to receive and our ability to impart it to others. Christ says, 'Everyone that asketh receiveth, and he that seeketh findeth' [Luke 11:10, 13b]. He who truly seeks for the precious grace of Christ, will be **sure** not to be disappointed.... We can be **assured** that we shall receive the Holy Spirit if we individually try the experiment of testing God's word.[2]

Sounds easy does it not? Beware, however, of overlooking that easily missed adverb, "truly." There is quite a gulf, it turns out, between "truly seeks" and "merely seeks." The use of the expression "truly seeks" suggests that there may be seeking of a different kind. That is indeed the case.

> We are to strive, to agonize, to enter in at the strait gate, for many shall *seek* to enter in, and shall not be able. It will take something more than mere *seeking* to enter in at the strait gate; for the gate to death is wide, and the road broad, and easy of access, and many there be that go in thereat [even while seeking to enter in at the strait gate!].[3]

---

[1] 2 Peter 3:9.

[2] *Review and Herald*, 5-5-1896, ¶ 1.

[3] *Ibid.*, 7-5-1892, ¶ 3. Italic added.

> Strive to enter in at the straight gate; for many ... will *seek*
> to enter in, and shall not be able.[1]

Thus that simple modifier, "truly," transforms "seeks" into "strives" or "agonizes" (to enter in), and warns us against seeking to make for ourselves and for others an easy, effortless, unobstructed freeway out of this world. Christ, through His Spirit, has designed and engineered that road, and the thirty-three and a half years Jesus spent upon this earth, including the closing scenes, clearly reveal its nature. Those who "agonize" to enter in are assured that they will not fail of receiving the needed grace of Christ. They are "assured that [they] shall receive the Holy Spirit," Who will, through enabling us to develop sound mental, physical, and spiritual habits, "finally make it easy."

> We should accustom ourselves to often lift the thoughts to
> God in prayer. If the mind wanders we must bring it back;
> by persevering effort, *habit will finally make it easy*.[2] We
> cannot for one moment separate ourselves from Christ with
> safety.[3]

Similar considerations apply to the word, "faith," and its power, or lack of it, to make available to us the effectiveness of the Holy Spirit's ministry in bringing to us enduring happiness and comfort. "Living, earnest, active faith" accomplishes this; but "casual faith," easy-chair faith, is powerless to make us rejoicing Christians or effective witnesses for Christ. Unfortunately, the latter is the "faith" that characterizes most so-called Christians.

---

[1] Luke 13:24. Italic added.

[2] Be slow to jump to the conclusion that the only behavior habitual "persevering effort" will make "easy" is prayer. Included is everything which helps preserve the attitude of prayer, or promotes a state of mind making us less inclined to "separate ourselves from Christ."

[3] *Review and Herald*, 11-15-1887. ¶ 11. Italic added. (Also found in *Amazing Grace*, 289; *Lift Him Up*, 144; *Messages to Young People*, 115; *Reflecting Christ*, 100, 295; *The Sanctified Life*, 93; and in several other places.)

[John 14:28, 12-14 quoted.] The faith here brought to view is not a casual faith; it is a living, earnest, active faith, that takes God at his word, and relies upon his pledged promises. This faith brings peace, and constitutes the children of God the light of the world.... It is enough to make the soul joyful to have such **assurances**—a Comforter always with us, and we revealing to the world in hopefulness, in joyfulness, that we have been called out of darkness into his marvelous light.[1]

♦ Further discussion on the relationship between faith and assurance may be found in Chapter 10 under the topic, "Assurance and Confidence."

"We are living in the time of the Holy Spirit's power."[2] This has been true since Pentecost, the "early rain," and will be especially true in the time of the closing up of the gospel, during the "more abundant" latter rain, when the events of Pentecost "are to be repeated, and with greater power."[3]

We have the **assurance** that in this age of the world the Holy Spirit will work with mighty power, unless by our unbelief we limit our blessing, and thus lose the advantages we might obtain.[4]

Is it possible for us to be assured that we are being possessed and illuminated by this mighty Power, and if so, how may we know?

If you delight to dwell upon the plan of salvation, upon the glorious manifestations of the divine character, if your heart, in contemplation of the love of God, glows with thankfulness and joy, **you may be sure** that you have been illuminated by the beams of the Holy Spirit.[5]

---

[1] *Signs of the Times,* 12-7-1891, ¶ 1.

[2] *Review and Herald,* 8-25-1896, ¶ 9.

[3] *Christ's Object Lessons,* 121.

[4] *Review and Herald,* 2-7-1957, ¶ 1 (Ms 148, 1899).

[5] *Signs of the Times,* 3-27-1893 ¶ 6. This statement appears with more of its context under the topic, "Assurance of Conversion," above.

> [T]rue light shines from God's word upon all hearts that are open to receive its precious rays; and it is your privilege to say, 'I **know** that my Redeemer liveth' [Job 19:25]. The Spirit will bear witness with your spirit that you are indeed children of God [Romans 8:16].[1]

If the above experience is not ours, is there anything we can *do* to obtain this inestimable blessing? The answer is clearly, yes. Above it was noted that we can limit our reception of this blessing by failing to exercise faith. Furthermore, as discussed above, we must surrender ourselves to be "guided and controlled by" the Holy Spirit if we are to have a part in the outpouring of the latter rain; we must ask for it. This is part of the necessary process of exercising faith.

> Ask, and it shall be given unto you.... If ye ... know how to give good gifts unto your children, How much more shall your heavenly Father give the Holy Spirit to them that ask him? —Luke 11:9, 13.

> At [man's] best and fullest, his own power is small. But to him who has entirely surrendered his life to God, the **assurance** is given that the Holy Spirit will be his helper. Jesus said, 'Ye shall receive power after that the Holy Ghost is come upon you' [Acts 1:8].[2]

◆ For related discussion on this subject see the topic, "Assurance and the Holy Spirit," in Chapter 10.

17. ASSURANCE OF VICTORY

Victory can be won only if we have superhuman power, because we are in conflict with a supernatural enemy to whom much power is provided, and who is not hesitant to exercise that power in ways which the Provider disapproves, but nevertheless allows. But power of itself cannot guarantee victory; power was available to Adam and

---

[1] *Review and Herald,* 11-9-1886, ¶ 16.

[2] *Ibid.,* 6-16-96, ¶ 4.

Eve in the beginning, but they did not prevail. Power must be skillfully applied. Examples of this abound in the Scriptures—Joshua at Gibeon; Gideon against the vast host of the Midianites; David against Goliath; Jonathan against the Philistine army at Michmash; Elijah versus Ahab and the prophets of Baal on Mount Carmel; Elisha and "death in the pot,"[1] and later surrounded by the Syrian host at Dothan; Hananiah, Mishael, and Azariah facing Nebuchadnezzar's superheated furnace; Daniel against the lions in Babylon; Peter in prison, sleeping like a baby the night before his scheduled execution; Paul, calmly sitting down to eat, while the ship on which he was prisoner was threatened with breaking up at any moment, and as he faced Nero's as-wielding executioner; John in the caldron of boiling oil, &c.

These conflicts were all characterized by two factors—superhuman power accompanied by an ingenious and economical application of that power. (If a fly was to be killed, a sledge hammer wasn't used; if a bear was to be caught, a mousetrap wasn't employed.) Man must take hold of the hand that is extended from heaven to help.

> Thy right hand, O Lord, is become glorious in power.... Strong is thy hand.... [The Lord's] right hand and his holy arm hath gotten him the victory.... The right hand of the Lord doeth valiantly.... Thy right hand shall save me.... I will strengthen thee ... with the right hand of my righteousness.[2]

Both the power and the ingenuity are supplied by that "hand" working through created beings—sometimes through unfallen beings with minimal human participation (as in the cases of Daniel and Peter), sometimes with major human participation (as with Elisha, Gideon, and David). "Let thy hand be upon the man of thy right hand ... whom thou

---

[1] 2 Kings 4:40, 41.

[2] Exodus 15:6; Psalms 89:13; 98:1; 118:15; 138:7; Isaiah 41:10.

madest strong,"[1] but always in association with the exercise of faith on the part of human beings. Faith is essential. But "when the Son of man cometh shall he find faith on the earth?"[2] The answer to that question is why so few find victory even though so much power, "all power," is available—for the asking.

> It is by a living faith in his power to help, that we shall receive strength to fight the battles of the Lord with the confident **assurance** of victory....
>
> We are not to rest quietly, with the thought that the devil will have nothing to do with us; but we can have the **assurance** that we shall not be left helpless, to be overcome by him.[3]

Such "confident assurance of victory" without a trace of anxiousness is exemplified in the experiences of many scriptural personages, many of which have already been mentioned. But the best example of all has not yet been considered—the incomparable, imperturbable Man, Christ Jesus. He could not be frightened or panicked by anything men or devils could devise. And by God's powerful grace such tranquil assurance of victory may characterize all of us who believe and follow Him. His Spirit is available—for the asking!

> In His humanity, perfected by a life of constant resistance of evil, the Saviour showed that through cooperation with Divinity, human beings may in this life attain to perfection of character. This is God's **assurance** to us that we too may obtain complete victory.[4]
>
> [God] sees the humble, trusting souls drawing near to Him, and in pity and love He draws near to them, and lifts up for

---

[1] Psalm 80:17.

[2] Luke 18:8.

[3] *Review and Herald*, 7-9-1908. ¶ 7. 15 (Sermon. 3-7-1908).

[4] *The Acts of the Apostles*. 531.

them a standard against the enemy. "Touch them not," He says, "for they are mine. I have graven them upon the palms of my hands" [Isaiah 49:16]. He teaches them to exercise unquestioning faith in His power to work in their behalf. With **assurance** they say, "This is the victory that overcometh the world, even our faith." 1 John 5:4.[1]

Nothing can "touch" them—no bullet, radiation, microbe, blast, careening drunk driver, avalanche, earthquake, tornado, flood, savage beast, gangster, rapist, mob, poison, &c. *ad infinitum*—without God's approval! We can be thankful for everything He approves. What a life!

18. ASSURANCE OF A (VERY) PERSONAL SAVIOUR

God has reminded us many times and in many ways of how *personal* salvation is. Salvation brings us into a personal relationship with Him, a closeness with which nothing else makes an adequate comparison. We have already elaborated to some extent upon this closeness under the topic in Chapter 2, "Assurance of an Intimately Present, Abiding Christ." Actually this incredibly close and personal experience to which the saving grace of God introduces us defies description. God has given us a glimpse into this personal relationship in His name which He told to Moses— "I AM." Jesus re-emphasized this concept. I AM the living water;[2] therefore drink Me in and be refreshed, nothing else can satisfy your thirst for fellowship. Wash in Me: "Wash you, make you clean."[3] I AM the bread of life.[4] Bread is made for one purpose—to eat, and we *are* what we eat.[5] It is as if we had eaten His flesh and blood[6] and He had been

---

[1] *Our High Calling*, 85. Cf. *Review and Herald*, 4-25-1907, ¶ 19.

[2] John 4:10-14.

[3] Isaiah 1:16.

[4] John 6:48-51.

[5] "We are composed of what we eat." —*Testimonies for the Church*, I, 682.

[6] John 6:53, 54.

diffused through our entire being, making us like Himself—Christlike—through and through, creating in us His own mind,[1] so that we love what and whom He loves and hate what He hates. I AM with you always—as both God and man, as both Creator and creature, as friend and spouse. Although man is gregarious in nature, and "the assembling of ourselves together"[2] is most enjoyable and profitable, we need never be depressed by loneliness, or deprived of divine or human companionship; you have both in Me, says Jesus. Right now—at this very moment *I AM*. I want to get *personal* with you!

> To eat the flesh and drink the blood of Christ is to receive Him as a personal Saviour,[3] believing that He forgives our sins, and that we are complete in Him [Colossians 2:10]. ... What food is to the body, Christ must be to the soul. Food cannot benefit us ... unless it becomes a part of our being. So Christ is of no value to us if we do not know Him as a personal Saviour.... We must feed upon Him, receive Him into the heart, so that His life becomes our life. His love, His grace, must be assimilated.... The experiences related in God's word are to be *my* experiences....
>
> God will make the most precious revelations to His hungering, thirsting people. They will find that Christ is a personal Saviour. As they feed upon His word, they find that it is spirit and life.[4]
>
> We must regard the Bible as addressed to us personally.[5]
>
> There is danger of not making Christ's teachings a personal matter, of not receiving them as though they were addressed to us personally.[6]

---

[1] 1 Corinthians 2:16.

[2] Hebrews 10:25.

[3] "Except ye eat the flesh of the Son of Man and drink his blood, ye have no [eternal] life in you. Whoso eateth my flesh and drinketh my blood hath eternal life." —John 6:53, 54.

[4] *The Desire of Ages*, 391.

[5] *Review and Herald*, 7-7-1891, ¶ 5.

[6] *Ibid.*, 7-22-1884, ¶ 20.

The Scriptures are to be received as God's word to us, not written merely, but spoken.... In them He is speaking to us individually, *speaking as directly as if we could listen to His voice.*[1]

In thus receiving the Saviour, eating and drinking His flesh and blood, drinking in the water of life, experiencing the experiences related in God's word, receiving the word as spoken to him personally, as though there were not another person in the world, the sinner participates in "working out [his] own salvation."[2] Thus he becomes yoked up with Jesus[3] as Jesus works out with him this intimate, personal, saving relationship. This relationship becomes more and more personal and intimate as the growing Christian progresses toward mature perfection—spiritual adulthood— (as distinguished from immature perfection—spiritual childhood). Mark presents this metaphorically: "First the blade, then the ear, after that the full corn in the ear."[4]

Man is given the privilege of working with God in the saving of his own soul. He is to receive Christ as his personal Saviour and believe in him. Receiving and believing is his part of the contract.[5]

All righteous attributes of character dwell in God as a perfect, harmonious whole. Every one who receives Christ as his personal Saviour is privileged to possess these attributes.... How glorious are the possibilities set before the fallen race![6]

From the above counsel we should be able to gain some assurance of how personal is to be our relationship to Jesus our Saviour, and from this understanding

---

[1] *The Ministry of Healing,* 122. Italic added.
[2] Philippians 2:12.
[3] Matthew 11:28-30.
[4] Mark 4:28.
[5] *Review and Herald,* 5-28-1908, ¶ 10.
[6] *Signs of the Times,* 9-3-1902, ¶ 1.

formulate a conclusion as to whether we have entered into a *saving* personal relationship with Him. We should either be assured that Jesus is not only *the* Saviour but *my* Saviour, or that we yet need to partake of this great gift—salvation— which Jesus offers to us *personally.* Jesus' gift of salvation is the personal gift of himself, His *Person,* to *me,* to die with me who am "dead in trespasses and sins."[1] I then rise from the dead with Him Who is "the Resurrection and the Life,"[2] to walk in newness of life, His life[3] forever to be united to Him.

Before we leave this subject we present evidence as to how "glorious" (as mentioned above) is this experience of having a personal saving relationship with Christ, and how much greater are our privileges in this respect than were those of God's people in ancient times.

> Our privileges are far greater than were the privileges of the Jews.... They had the Old Testament history; we have that and the New Testament also. We have the **assurance** of a Saviour who *has* come—a Saviour who *has* been crucified, *has* risen, and *has* proclaimed over the rent sepulcher of Joseph, "I am the resurrection, and the life." In our knowledge of Jesus and his love, the kingdom of God has been placed in the midst of us [Matthew 18:20; Luke 17:21].... We have had presented to us by the messengers of God the richest feast—the righteousness of Christ, justification by faith, the exceeding great and precious promises of God in his word, free access to the Father by Jesus Christ, the comforts of the Holy Spirit, and the well-grounded **assurance** of eternal life in the kingdom of God.[4]

> A more clear and glorious light [than shone in Old Testament times] now shines upon the Christian.... What

---

[1] Ephesians 2:1.
[2] John 11:25
[3] Romans 6:4-11.
[4] *Review and Herald,* 1-17-1899. ¶ 13. Emphases added.

had to be grasped by faith by them is **assurance** to us; for we know that Christ has come as foretold by the prophets.[1]

[Y]ou say, If I could only **know** that he is my Saviour! Well, what kind of evidence do you want? Do you want a special feeling or emotion to prove that Christ is yours? Is this more reliable than pure faith in God's promises?[2]

♦   For more discussion of "Assurance and Feeling" see this topic in chapter 10.

There are other ways by which we may be assured that we have truly entered into a personal, saving relationship with the Saviour, methods by which we may examine ourselves whether we are in the faith.[3]   One of these is to examine where our loyalties lie:

Let this point be fully settled in every mind: If we accept Christ as a Redeemer, *we must accept Him as a Ruler.* We cannot have the **assurance** and perfect confiding trust in Christ as our Saviour until we acknowledge Him as our King and are obedient to His commandments.[4]

God does not intend that we shall be left in doubt about this matter. He intends that we shall know of a certainty of our standing before Him.

Christ is our present, all-sufficient Saviour. In him all fulness dwells. It is the privilege of Christians to **know** that Christ is in them of a truth.[5]

This knowledge fills the mind with peace, rest-producing, health-giving peace—that passes all understanding.[6]

---

[1] *Signs of the Times,* 2-20-1893, ¶ 3.

[2] *Review and Herald,* 7-29-1890, ¶ 6.

[3] 2 Corinthians 13:5.

[4] *Faith and Works,* 16 (Ms 36, 1890). Emphases added.

[5] *Signs of the Times,* 9-2-1897, ¶ 14.

[6] Philippians 4:7.

ASSURANCE OF WHAT?

> When we individually rest upon Christ, with **full assurance**
> of faith, trusting alone to the efficacy of his blood to cleanse
> from all sin, we shall have peace in believing that what God
> has promised he is able to perform.[1]

God wants all men to know that they are loved by Him. It is the privilege of those who have accepted Jesus as their personal Saviour to have such an assurance and for others to be able to recognize also that those who are God's are loved by Him. "Love begets love, affection begets affection"[2] This is a glorious experience that can be distinctly sensed when one realizes that love for him is arising in someone else's heart and a heart-warming response is arising in his own heart. See the topic, "Assurance of Love," for more on this love relationship.

We should certainly *know* that Jesus is our personal Saviour!—if He is.

The thing that puts distance between God and ourselves is sin. We have an internal awareness that we are incapable of coping with the natural forces that threaten to cause the disintegration of the world about us, and with the supernatural forces that are against us which, though unseen, we suspect all too well are there. Therefore the farther we get from God, the more vulnerable and insecure we feel. The Scriptures are clear on this:

> The Lord's hand is not shortened, that it cannot save;
> neither his ear heavy, that it cannot hear; but your iniquities
> have separated between you and your God, and your sins
> have hid his face from you.[3]

One of the great accomplishments of salvation is to guarantee security and freedom from fear, conflict, and anxiety forever.

---

[1] *Review and Herald,* 3-5-1889, ¶ 6 (South Lancaster, 1-11-1889).

[2] *Testimonies for the Church,* II, 95; *The Desire of Ages,* 519.

[3] Isaiah 59:1, 2.

There is no necessity for any follower of Christ to have any uncertainty about the future.

Just as we must die and be born anew every day[1] so these assurances, this peace, this freedom from uncertainty is to be renewed daily.

> We are not obliged to trust in the evidence that we had a year or a month ago, but we may have the **assurance** *today* that Jesus lives, and is making intercession for us.[2]

And because, through this saving death and re-creation experience with Jesus—He in me and I in Him—I live also. I am privileged to have the assurance that my life, although perhaps characterized by a period of sleep, can no more be terminated than can His. As the ears of my spiritual being have been alert—as were the ears of the five wise virgins of Matthew 25—to hear His lightest whisper, so will I, whether waking or sleeping, whether walking the earth or entombed within it, whether sailing the sea or buried beneath its waves, always be within earshot of Jesus, and responsive to His every call.

---

[1] 1 Corinthians 15:31.

[2] *Review and Herald*, 4-22-1884, ¶ 11 (1883 General Conference). Emphases added.

Chapter 5
ASSURANCE OF A GROWING EXPERIENCE

19. ASSURANCE THAT CHRIST HAS COME

God's people today accept Christ's first coming, two millenniums ago, without question. What the ancients were obligated to receive by faith, we believe by "sight." But whether He has come into *my* heart *personally* is another matter. The life styles of few who believe in the birth of Jesus, the Messiah, in Bethlehem indicate that they have received Him as a personal, life-changing Saviour, born in their hearts, Whose second appearing in glory is imminent.

> A more clear and glorious light [than shone in Old Testament times] now shines upon the Christian.... [W]hat had to be grasped by faith by them is **assurance** to us; for we know that Christ has come as foretold by the prophets. It is just as essential for us to have faith in our Redeemer [who has come and will come again] ... as it was for the ancients to believe in a Redeemer to come, represented by their offerings and sacrifices.[1]

---

[1] *Signs of the Times,* 2-20-1893. ¶ 3.

20. ASSURANCE THAT WEAKNESSES MAY BECOME STRENGTHS

If there is anything that characterizes the human race in this age it is weakness. From material considerations there has never been such a powerful and knowledgeable people upon the earth. In weaponry, transportation, communication, computation, conveniences, &c, no previous generation has stood near the present generation. But in spiritual matters, "knowledge has decreased with every successive generation upon the earth";[1] "every generation takes up some phase of evil in advance of the one which preceded it."[2] By this unprecedented power and because of this unprecedented weakness Satan stalks about devouring almost at will.[3] But mankind has not been left in these threatening circumstances without help. This spine-tingling remedy is what this section is about.

> [Men and women through faith] out of weakness were made strong.[4]

> My grace is sufficient for thee: for my strength is made perfect in weakness.[5]

> He giveth power to the faint; and to them that have no might he increaseth strength.[6]

There is a condition that must be met if our weakness is to be transformed into strength—clinging to the inspired word of God, where the principles of truth and power may be found:

---

[1] *Spiritual Gifts*, IVa, 154.

[2] *Review and Herald*, 4-16-1901, ¶ 8.

[3] 1 Peter 5:8.

[4] Hebrews 11:34.

[5] 2 Corinthians 12:9.

[6] Isaiah 40:29.

He who steadfastly adheres to the principles of truth has the **assurance** that his weakest points of character may become his strongest points.[1]

Jesus said, "The truth shall make you free."[2] And the Psalmist wrote, "I will walk at liberty, for I seek thy precepts."[3] It requires great power to free from bondage one who is imprisoned by a mighty foe. These scriptures make it plain that such power comes through the "truth," the inspired "precepts." If we steadfastly cling to the word of God, we will find the mysterious, supernatural weapons that will enable us to "resist" and drive off our powerful enemy.

When we resist the devil, he will flee from us [James 4:7], and we will rise above the human weakness in a way that will be a mystery even to ourselves.[4]

There is ... no weakness but he can change to power.[5]

21. ASSURANCE OF GROWTH

As newborn babes, desire the sincere milk of the word, that ye may grow thereby.[6]

Grow in grace, and in the knowledge of our Lord and Saviour Jesus Christ.[7]

The same Spirit also uses this same metaphor of the milk to reprove some of the Hebrews for a failure to make spiritual growth *beyond* infancy:

When for the time ye ought to be teachers, ye have need that one teach you again which be the first principles of the

---

[1] *Review and Herald*, 2-18-1904, ¶ 10.

[2] John 8:32.

[3] Psalm 119:45.

[4] *Signs of the Times*, 10-29-1894, ¶ 9.

[5] *Review and Herald*, 1-14-1890, ¶ 6.

[6] 1 Peter 2:2.

[7] 2 Peter 3:18.

oracles of God; and are become such as have need of milk, and not of strong meat. For everyone that useth milk is unskillful in the word of righteousness; for he is a babe. But strong meat belongeth to them that are of full age.... Therefore ... let us go on unto perfection.[1]

There is no conflict here. The apostle asserts that we cannot stop growing and be saved. We must get beyond the infant stage, beyond being babes in the truth. We are not always to be occupied with "*first* principles." We do not have the option of growing or not growing. We cannot remain spiritual infants. We must grow or die. We must "go on unto [maturity]." To choose to remain in spiritual infancy is to choose eternal death. The choice is ours.

[T]he development of the plant is a beautiful figure of Christian growth. As in nature, so in grace; there can be no life without growth. The plant must either grow or die.... At every stage of development our life may be perfect; yet if God's purpose for us is fulfilled, there will be continual advancement.[2]

When the plant stops reaching for the sun it dies. When finite man stops reaching for, and becoming more like, the Sun of Righteousness, he begins to die, and will eventually wither away into eternal nothingness. The goal before us— now and through all eternity—for which we reach is nothing less than "the measure of the stature of the fulness of Christ."

Till we all come in the unity of the faith, and of the knowledge of the Son of God, unto a perfect man, unto the measure of the stature of the fulness of Christ, that we henceforth be no more children, tossed to and fro, and carried about with every wind of doctrine ... but speaking the truth in love, may grow up into him in all things, which is the head, even Christ.[3]

---

[1] Hebrews 5:12-6:1

[2] *Christ's Object Lessons,* 65.

[3] Ephesians 4:13-15.

ASSURANCE OF WHAT?

The Holy Spirit elaborates further upon the details of this process:

> Add to your faith virtue; and to virtue knowledge; and to knowledge temperance; and to temperance patience; and to patience godliness; and to godliness brotherly kindness, and to brotherly kindness charity.... If ye do these things, ye shall never fall.[1]

To reiterate, we must grow or die. We cannot stand still. Everything living—or dying—in the natural world about us illustrates this, so that if we fail to understand this important principle, we are "without excuse."[2] As in the natural, so in the spiritual; we are progressing in the upward path, or retrograding. Salvation is a contract. Man's part in this contract is "receiving and believing."[3] But one cannot take in (receive) without giving out, because man is not a reservoir but a conduit—the rate of intake is controlled by the rate of output. There are many appropriate metaphors—the plant takes in carbon dioxide to give forth oxygen, without which nothing could live; precipitation and evaporation; the tree's taking in nutrients and giving fruit; a pipe receives water at the spring as the faucet gives out water, *et cetera*. This implies that *giving*, as well as "receiving," is a "part of the contract," an essential component of the growth process.

> Wherever there is life, there is increase and growth; in God's kingdom there is a constant interchange—taking in and giving out; receiving and returning to the Lord His own.... If truth does not flow forth from [the receiver] to others, he loses his capacity to receive. We must impart the goods of heaven if we desire fresh blessings.[4]

---

[1] 2 Peter 1:5-7, 10.

[2] Romans 1:20.

[3] "[John 1:12 quoted.] If man could appreciate this great blessing, what an advantage it would be to him! He is given the privilege of being a laborer together with God in the saving of his soul. Receiving and believing is his part of the contract." *Review and Herald*, 4-24-1900. ¶ 3.

[4] *Testimonies for the Church*, VI, 448.

An illustration of this no-life-without-growth concept may be found in your garden. I have had some small successes in growing fine watermelons year after year to share with our neighbors. The spring of 1997, however, was very slow in turning into summer. After we had transplanted the tiny seedlings into the out-of-doors in mid-May, thinking that in about eleven or twelve weeks we would have delicious fruit on the vines, the weather failed to warm up as expected. The plants made no growth for several weeks. Two weeks to recover from transplant shock is normal, but when there was no evidence of growth for twice that long, our feelings of assurance changed into concern.

As the plants failed to grow they looked more and more bedraggled, and we sadly realized they were slowly dying and would soon have to be plowed under. Then we had several warm, sunny days, and the plants quickly began to put on new foliage. We reaped the results in about sixty delightful watermelons to share with those about us. The plants did not spread out as far as usual, the harvest was later, and the number of melons was about two-thirds normal; but the flavor was as good as ever.

Since *making growth* in the likeness of God is so vital to the Christian, God has assured us of its possibility, and of His full assistance in accomplishing man's continuing growth.

A five-months-old baby girl (or boy) is a darling little person. She is about twice her birth-weight, and we love her smiles, her miniature hands and feet, her efforts to talk. Even though she may to all appearances be perfect, we would be greatly concerned if, seven months later, there had been no change, no growth. By now she should be becoming a small child three times her birth-weight, learning to walk, saying a few recognizable words, eating more foods from the table. So with spiritual matters;

a lack of growth should be a matter of distress to all concerned with the nurture of new-born babes in the faith.

> [U]nless the Christian continues to grow, he will retrograde, and his experience will become sickly and be fruitless of good.[1]

> God designs that Christians shall grow continually—grow up unto the full stature of men and women in Christ. All who do not grow stronger, and become more firmly rooted and grounded in the truth, are continually retrograding.[2]

The process is not a hard one to master, no more difficult than growing good watermelons. As with the watermelons, man's part is made simple so that the process is an easy one to learn and execute. All the complicated, difficult processes, which are many, are done by the great heavenly Master Gardener.

> Many are longing to grow in grace.... The Master has given them a work to do whereby they shall grow.... [J]ust do every duty that presents itself, carry the burden of souls on your heart, and by every conceivable means seek to save the lost.[3]

Furthermore, as we near the end of this world's history, God assures us that we may expect an acceleration in the rate of spiritual growth on the part of every Christian, both those newly born and those of more mature age.

> [A]s we near the close of this earth's history we advance *more and more rapidly* in Christian growth, or we retrograde just as decidedly.[4]

---

[1] *Signs of the Times*, 4-3-1893, ¶ 2.

[2] *Testimonies for the Church*, IV, 556.

[3] *Youth's Instructor*, 2-3-1898, ¶ 3.

[4] *That I May Know Him*, 117 (1890).

This increasing rate of spiritual growth reaches breathtaking speed just before the great "time of trouble" predicted by the Scriptures,[1] breaks upon our world.

> It is too late in the day to feed with milk. If souls *a month or two* old[!] in the truth, who are about to enter the time of trouble such as never was, cannot hear all the straight truth, or endure the strong meat of the straightness of the way, how will they stand in the day of battle? Truths that we have been years learning must be learned *in a few months* by those who now embrace the Third Angel's Message.... There is no need of milk after souls are convinced of the truth.... It is a disgrace for those who have been in the truth for years to talk of feeding souls who have been *months* in the truth, upon milk. It shows they know little of the leadings of the Spirit of the Lord, and realize not the time we are living in. Those who embrace the truth now will have to step fast.[2]

The growth so dramatically portrayed in the previous paragraph is not in numbers or material assets. Those things will take care of themselves when there is growth in *grace,* in Christlikeness that results from the ingestion of the strong meat of the word of God.

There are those who believe that growth ends with glorification, or perhaps even with the sealing work described in Revelation 7:1-3; but God has assured us that He does not agree with this view.

> The Lord does not design that we shall ever feel that we have reached to the full measure of the stature of Christ. *Through all eternity* we are to grow in knowledge of Him who is the head of all things in the church.[3]

> To dwell forever in this home of the blest, to bear in soul, body, and spirit ... the perfect likeness of our Creator, and

---

[1] Daniel 12:1.

[2] *Manuscript Releases,* I, 33, 34 (1854). Italic added.

[3] *Signs of the Times,* 5-9-1892, ¶ 8. Italic added.

through ceaseless ages to advance in wisdom, in knowledge, and in holiness, ever exploring new fields of thought, ever finding new wonders and new glories, ever increasing in capacity to know and to enjoy and to love, and knowing that there is still beyond us joy and love and wisdom infinite—such is the object to which the Christian's hope is pointing.[1]

Continued spiritual growth in grace is a key secret of security in the Christian's experience. The apostle Peter affirms that we are secure from falling as long as we are growing. The spiritual plant must cease to grow before it can die!

[Peter] drew attention to the precious privileges within the reach of every believer.... "Give diligence," he pleaded, "to make your calling and election **sure**; for if ye do these things [keep advancing up the growth ladder of verses 5-7], ye shall never fall; for so an entrance shall be ministered unto you abundantly into the everlasting kingdom of our Lord and Saviour Jesus Christ" [2 Peter 1:10, 11]. Precious **assurance**! Glorious is the hope before the believer as he advances by faith toward the heights of Christian perfection![2]

♦ See Chapter 10, under "Assurance and Maturity," for more on this topic.

22. ASSURANCE OF CHRIST'S RIGHTEOUSNESS

Christ's righteousness—like the infilling of the Holy Spirit—provides us with all the assurances discussed in this book. And furthermore we are assured that we may have this priceless gift of His righteousness. "Righteousness is right-doing,"[3] and therefore the righteousness of Christ is the right-doing of Christ, inwardly and outwardly—motivationally and behaviorally. The Holy Spirit speaks to us concerning this as follows:

---

[1] *Counsels to Parents, Teachers, and Students*, 55. Italic added.

[2] *The Acts of the Apostles*, 533.

[3] *Christ's Object Lessons*, 312.

> Having therefore ... boldness to enter into the holiest
> [*holies*—Greek] by the blood of Jesus by a new and *living*
> way ... through the veil, that is to say, his flesh ... let us
> draw near with a true heart in full **assurance** of faith, having
> our hearts sprinkled from an evil conscience and our bodies
> washed with pure water.[1]

This text is very deep and important to us. "His flesh" is the
"veil" between God and ourselves. God is on one side, and
we on the other. In order to be saved we must pass through
this veil, the flesh of our Lord Jesus Christ. After the feeding
of the "five thousand," Jesus plainly taught that, if we would
have eternal life—that is, be saved—we must "eat" our way
through that veil, *the Word of God.*

> Jesus said ... Except ye eat the flesh of the Son of man, and
> drink his blood, ye have no [eternal] life in you. Whoso
> eateth my flesh, and drinketh my blood, hath eternal life....
> The *words* that I speak unto you ... they are [eternal] life.[2]

If we are to be saved, the robe of Christ's righteousness must,
most importantly, be *taken in*—"eaten"—as well as *put on.*
The Bible plainly teaches that only those who have put on the
garments of Christ's righteousness are saved. What we have
seen here is that this salvation *experience* is a complete
inward and outward transformation into the likeness of
Christ. "Ye are complete in him."[3] The word of God in our
hands is a most wonderful assurance that every person of
reasoning powers may meet these conditions.

The man without the wedding garment of Matthew 22:11-14,
lacked more than an outward change! The inward *and*
outward manifestations of saving grace are inseparable.
Thus Jesus can say, "By their fruits ye shall know them."[4]

---

[1] Hebrews 10:19, 20, 22.

[2] John 6:53, 54, 63. Italic added. (The entire passage, vss. 47-63, is most instructive.)

[3] Colossians 2:10.

[4] Matthew 7:20.

When the King came into the wedding feast He could immediately discern who were prepared to sit down to the feast with Him in the kingdom of God. He could simply look at their clothing! Were their lives characterized by right-doing—Christ's righteousness—or were their actions following threads and motives of their own devising, of human origin? "All will be justified by their faith, and judged by their works,"[1] *a books transaction.* Salvation is "by grace ... through faith,"[2] but judgment is by works! Saving faith produces good works, and so if there are no good works, there is no saving faith.

It is important to observe here that if my wedding clothing is woven of threads of my own devising, by which I am to be judged, that garment reveals my life history, as well as my current behavior. Thus in the judgment accurate conclusions can be formulated from the cumulative works history. If that history, particularly its record of *wrong*-doing, has been blotted out by the blood of Christ—covered (hidden) by His righteousnes, His *right*-doing—then a negative judgment cannot be supported. Hallelujah!

This fact that saving faith is always productive of good works so that in the judgment no one need be asked what he *believes,* but only what he has *done,* enables us to tell something now about what the decision will be then: "Examine yourselves, whether ye be in the faith."[3] N.B.: we are not encouraged to examine *others*: "let a man examine *himself.*"[4] It is entirely appropriate for me to examine someone else's "works" to determine if I should marry him, hire him, vote for him, make him my roommate, a business partner, the head deaconess, *et cetera*; but *never* to determine

---

[1] *Testimonies for the Church,* IV, 386.

[2] Ephesians 2:8.

[3] 2 Corinthians 13:5.

[4] 1 Corinthians 11:28.

whether he is "in the faith." This means that when the local church—with perfect propriety—votes someone out of office or membership in the *local body*—or refuses to accept someone into its membership—it is making no statement about the current status of the involved individual's name in Heaven's *Book of Life*.

> We are to put into practice the precepts of the law, and thus have righteousness before us; the rearward will be God's glory. The light of the righteousness of Christ will be our front guard, and the glory of the Lord will be our rearward [Isaiah 58:8]. Let us thank the Lord for this **assurance**."[1]

23. ASSURANCE OF POWER

> Let him take hold of my strength, that he may make peace with me; and he shall make peace with me.[2]

> Thine is the ... power ... forever.[3]

> *All* power is given unto me.[4]

> Thou couldest have no power at all ... except it were given thee from above.[5]

> God hath not given us the spirit of fear; but of power ... love ... and ...a sound mind.[6]

> All *things* come of thee.[7]

Things" here is understood to include the intangible, such as abstract ideas. It requires power to think! All power and authority flow from God. Without power an "authority" is nothing but a figurehead without any means by

---

[1] *Selected Messages*, 1, 99 (1-23-1904) (Also in *Notebook Leaflets*, "The Church," No. 7).

[2] Isaiah 27:5.

[3] Matthew 6:13.

[4] Matthew 28:18. Italic added.

[5] John 19:11.

[6] 2 Timothy 1:7.

[7] 1 Chronicles 29:14. Italic added.

which his so-called authority may be enforced. It requires power to use, to control power.[1] Given sufficient power, one also has authority; and given all power, he has all rule-making, behavior-controlling authority. The only ones exempted from such rules—authority—are those who are the source of power, and therefore have greater power. They can "shut your water off" at will! Be thankful that we have an all-powerful *and* a benevolent, reassuring God!

> [W]hen he saith all things are put under him, it is manifest that he is excepted, which did put all things under him.[2]

We may then conclude that when Jesus said, "All power [authority] is *given* unto me," His Father is the Source of that power and is not under that authority, and that there are no exceptions in the creation.

For the most part in this writing, "power" is used for both of the concepts, power and authority, assuming that power is being discussed in the context of its intelligent use.

The six scripture references at the beginning of this topic show that all power, *even that which empowers evil purposes* (John 19:11), comes from God. This has very broad implications. For example, it requires that everywhere power is manifested, the immediate, full involvement of God is required—a staggering concept when one realizes some of its implications. There are no secondary, independent dynamos in the universe that would exist in the absence of God's immediate involvement—not a particle of matter, not a cell or atom or energy wave! *"All* things come of thee." In the age of modern physics, even many non-scientists are

---

[1] For those who have concerns about this regress of power required to control power, and therefore power to control the power that controls the power, &c.—like Borden's evaporated milk cans which had a framed picture of Elsie the cow in a pastoral setting containing a can of Borden's evaporated milk, which had a reduced reproduction of the same picture including a can of Borden's evaporated milk, which had ... &c., supposedly ad infinitum—let us say that the controlling power regress, ends fairly quickly at the Source of all power.

[2] 1 Corinthians 15:27.

aware that such unlikely participants as inanimate objects—
"things," all of which come from God—are ("concentrated")
energy—power—and so could not exist in the absence of the
immediate agency of God, because *all* power originates in
Him and cannot exist independently of Him.[1] We can
therefore say, "Without him was [and *is*] not anything made
[and maintained]." "By him were all things created, that *are*
in heaven, and that *are* in earth, visible and invisible." "In
him we live, and move, and have our being.."[2] Remove
God's presence from anything and it has no "being"
(existence).

> All *things* come of thee.

It may come as a disturbing surprise that implements
designed primarily to wound, destroy, or kill, such as an
arrow, sword, bullet, bomb, or missile, cannot function or
exist, cannot even leave the bow, scabbard, gun muzzle,
bomb bay, rocket launcher, apart from the agency of God.
Explosives cannot ignite, or exist. Guns cannot exist. The
hand or device that holds the weapon cannot raise it, release
the bow-string, draw the sword, squeeze the trigger, or even
exist without the immediate involvement of God.
Furthermore, once the bowstring twangs, the spear is hurled,
or the propellant ignites, the projectile cannot continue a
hairsbreadth on its way unless the "hand" of God is upon it,
moving it along as it were toward its target.[3] Remove that

---

[1] "It is not by inherent power that ... the earth yields its bounties, and continues its march around the sun. The *hand* of the Infinite One is perpetually at work guiding this planet. It is God's power *continually exercised* that keeps the earth in position in its rotation.... It is not as the result of a mechanism, which, once set in motion, continues its work, that the pulse beats, and breath follows breath.... The beating heart, the throbbing pulse, every nerve and muscle in the living organism, is kept in order and activity by the power of an *ever-present* God." —*The Ministry of Healing,* 416f. Italic added.

[2] John 1:3; Colossians 1:16; Acts 17:28. Italic added.

[3] It is perhaps desirable to elaborate here to some extent on a matter that while not the subject of this book, is closely related to it. One needs to differentiate carefully between empowering something's or someone's action and *responsibility* for that action. I attempt a most inadequate example. I have a friend who is building a house. He runs out of money. I loan him what he needs to complete his house, thus empowering him to finish the house; but I am not responsible for the kind of house he builds. I do not

influence and there is no longer in existence arrow, spear, bullet, bomb, or missile. The same power that brought the universe, along with these weapons, into existence continually keeps it in existence.[1]

Troubling? Yes, to some; but viewed differently it is most reassuring. In my youth (when I was a soldier during World War II) I took comfort in reciting texts like Psalm 34:7; an angel could intervene at any time in my behalf, make the bullets, the blasts, the shrapnel, the poison gas *miss* me! Thus I could be injured or killed *only by God's permission.* I still believe in such intervention, but it has taken on a new, still more reassuring dimension; I have an improved understanding of God's omnipotence, omniscience, omnipresence, His immediacy—something closer to a "first-cause" concept. God has more ways to help me:

---

stand by and supervise everything he does to be sure his house is according to my liking. That remains *his* choice.

The reason the example is so inadequate is that God's involvement in our actions is so much more intimate. His providing the power is not like putting money into your pocket or gasoline into your tank. It is putting something of Himself into your task. His hand is on yours as you pound every nail, lay every brick, install every switch. As you draw every plan His mind is connected to yours. He is immediately causing the gasoline to flow through the gas-line, to burn in the engine. Without His immediate involvement none of these—hand, builder, house blueprints, nails, bricks, gasoline, pipeline, engine, combustion could exist. These considerations have led some to deism, others to pantheism, still others to determinism, where man functions in some way independently of God, is God, or is simply God's puppet.

The marvelous, but baffling (to the finite mind), truth is that God in His omniscient omnipotence has created a universe in which there is *freedom of choice,* free moral agency, In which some of God's creatures share *with* Him in a most intimate and mysterious way, some of His infinite prerogatives. We can experience something of God! We will enter more and more into an understanding of this incredible privilege, this shared experience; but to grasp it fully will always be beyond us. But one thing needs to be held without wavering—God is not responsible for evil. "What was it caused **SATAN** to rebel? Was there any just reason that could be assigned for his sin? The place where sin originated has been pointed out, but the reason for sin cannot be found; for there is no reason for its existence." —*Signs of the Times,* 9-18-93, ¶ 3. God wishes us to believe that the creation of the possibility for sin was not the creation of sin.

[1] "The *same creative energy* that brought the world into existence is still exerted in upholding the universe and continuing the operations of nature." *Counsels to Parents, Teachers, and Students,* 185. Italic added. Cf. Colossians 1:16, 17. The entire created universe seems to be in a constant state of change, and the argument is not wholly without validity that the creation is from moment to moment in continual process of re-creation according to a specific plan. Remove God and the universe does not *over time* pass out of existence; it ceases to exist that very instant because it is not at that instant *created.*

Our heavenly Father has a *thousand* ways to provide for us, of which we know nothing.[1]

Furthermore:

One day is with the Lord as a thousand years.[2]

It isn't wise to read too much into any text of Scripture, but let us speculate just a moment upon Peter's brief statement, involving a somewhat different tack to the concept of the immediacy of God. Peter might as well have said (with some loss of symbolism), "One second is with the Lord as four days" (the proportions[3] are about the same). If it takes *one second* for a gun-slinger to draw and fire, it might seem that if I dart a prayer to heaven for help, God hasn't much time to intervene. But it is no emergency to God, no more than if He had *four days* in which to react. He could be quite unhurried! He could take care of a number of really important, major issues in the universe, and still have an abundance of time to intervene in my *small* (to Him) problem.

God is never hurried or under pressure! He knows no emergencies, no code-blue situations. There is never any panic in heaven over any of Satan's maneuvers! Consequently neither need there be any panic on our part! God's attention is never diverted from me, nor from the gunslinger, his hand, his gun, the bullet, its trajectory, &c *ad infinitum*. None of these "things," including the human beings involved, could so much as exist without God's "hand" being immediately upon them—that is, in the absence of the exercise, that very instant, of the creative power of God. "Our divine Lord is equal to any emergency"![4]

---

[1] *The Desire of Ages*, 330.

[2] 2 Peter 3:8.

[3] I would not wish anyone to conclude from this that I believe that the "proportions" in Peter's statement are his main thrust, or that he even had the concept of proportions in mind.

[4] *Review and Herald*, 6-9-1910, ¶ 2.

R elax, humankind! Cast off your frantic desperations! God has plenty of time (and power and know-how) to take care of all our needs, all of our so-called extremities![1] Furthermore, as previously implied above, for that bullet to accomplish the intent of the one who fired the gun the bullet must reach its target. But God's involvement with the projectile is essential at every millimeter of its progress; He must continually exercise His creative power to keep it in existence. Allow that to lapse, any inattention on God's part during any part of its trajectory, and the bullet cannot exist, much less reach its target. With God's full attention on both the target and the projectile, and with such a luxury of time as mortals seldom enjoy, be assured—there is no possibility of interference with His will.

But, you ask, what if there is insufficient time for *me* to react, to dart that prayer to heaven for help? One second is not like four days to *me*! God, in His omniscience, has already solved that problem as well. He knows our minds. If we are inclined to seek His help when in need, then He assures us that He will answer the prayer we would have sent heavenward, had we known of the need and had the time: "Before they call, I will answer."[2] God, in fact, is constantly in the business of answering the prayers of His children that are unoffered because of their lack of awareness of what is going on in this universe, their ignorance of the plans and activities of their enemies, natural or supernatural. God cannot be caught by surprise, and neither can I, if God is in me and I in Him. Because of His sufficiencies, my insufficiencies are no cause for fear or alarm![3]

---

[1] "[M]an's extremities are God's opportunities." —*Selected Messages*, II. 297.

[2] Isaiah 65:24.

[3] This is also the basis of of a very important matter we have no space to discuss further here— *righteousness by faith*. See, for example, Dennis E. Priebe's *Face to Face with the Real Gospel* (Nampa, ID: Pacific Press. 1985).

And His will is subject to His great love, mercy, and grace continually exercised toward us, the fallen race, the object of His supreme regard. Our enemy, Satan, may catch us sleeping, but he will never catch God sleeping. Satan's very existence (and ours) depends upon his never catching God sleeping! But us?—"What I say unto you I say unto all, Watch"![1]

> We have the **assurance** that in this age of the world the Holy Spirit will work with mighty power, unless by our unbelief we limit our blessing, and thus lose the advantages we might obtain.[2]

> [W]hen we submit to God's way, the Lord Jesus guides our minds and fills our lips with **assurance**. We may be strong in the Lord and in the power of His might. Receiving Christ, we are clothed with power.[3]

> We have an **assurance** that Jesus is our Saviour, and that we may draw freely from Him.... We may take Him at His word ... and know that He will give us grace and power to do just as He bids us.[4]

We are finite, and finiteness, wherever it is found, has strength only in proportion to its hold upon the Infinite. That is where faith gets involved. Through faith we may take control of some aspect of God's behavior and *require* that He give us the help that we need. He will not cast us off. Take hold, then, upon God—forcefully,[5] relentlessly,[6] refusing to let Him go,[7] He does not want us to let Him off the hook! What a God! In our weak strength, granted to us through

---

[1] Mark 13:37.

[2] *Review and Herald*, 2-7-1957, ¶ 1 (Ms 148, 1899).

[3] *Testimonies for the Church*, VII, 71.

[4] *Sermons and Talks*, II, 293 (Sermon, 3-10-1908).

[5] Matthew 11:12.

[6] Luke 11:5-13.

[7] Genesis 32:26.

grace,[1] exhausted in hanging onto God, we will be made partakers of infinite power, of the divine nature.[2] What incredible assurance!

> At his best and fullest, [man's] own power is small. But to him who has entirely surrendered his life to God, the **assurance** is given that the Holy Spirit will be his helper. Jesus said, 'Ye shall receive power after that the Holy Ghost is come upon you' [Acts 1:8].[3]

> It is by a living faith in his power to help, that we shall receive strength to fight the battles of the Lord with the confident **assurance** of victory.[4]

> To go forward without stumbling, we must have the **assurance** that a hand all-powerful will hold us up, and an infinite pity be exercised toward us if we fall.[5]

> The **assurance** that we are under the protection of Omnipotence imparts courage and **confidence**, inspires a hope that is "as an anchor of the soul, both sure and steadfast, and which entereth into that within the vail" [Hebrews 6:19]. This **assurance** is a source of strength unknown to the worldling or to the half-hearted professor.[6]

> It is the privilege of God's people to go forth to their work in the strength of Jesus. We should go forth, not depending upon our talents, but wrestling with God for sanctification through the truth. We should feel a constant **assurance** that Jesus is present to help us.[7]

> "God with us" [Matthew 1:23] is the **surety** of our deliverance from sin, the **assurance** of our power to obey the law of heaven.[8]

---

[1] 2 Corinthians 12:9.

[2] 2 Peter 1:4.

[3] *Review and Herald*, 6-16-1896, ¶ 4.

[4] *Ibid.*, 7-9-1908, ¶ 8 (sermon, 3-7-1908).

[5] *Signs of the Times*, 7-28-1881, ¶ 15.

[6] *Ibid.*, 1-28-1886, ¶ 10.

[7] *Ibid.*, 3-31-1890, ¶ 4.

[8] *The Desire of Ages*, 25.

Chapter 6
ASSURANCE OF CLEAR SPIRITUAL INSIGHT

24. ASSURANCE OF CLEAR VISION

Conversion prepares the way for the Holy Spirit to clear the cobwebs, the fog, from our spiritual vision. Before we are renewed in the image of Christ, so that "we have the mind of Christ"[1] nothing is clear—although it may seem so.[2] Revelation 3:17 asserts that not even our thinking about clearness is clear! But grace has provided a way out. Through grace God has provided a light at the end of the tunnel, an unobstructed window through which light shines into the darkened mind, pointing the way out of what is otherwise impenetrable darkness. Man may either follow this light, whose brightness increases as he continues in it, out of darkness to clear spiritual vision, or he may choose to pull down the curtain, turn his back to the light, and become involved in greater darkness and confusion about his own state of enlightenment until his darkness finally becomes impenetrable even by the light of God's grace. The apostle writes of this as follows:

> The invisible things of [God] from the creation of the world are clearly seen, being understood by the things that are made, even his eternal power and Godhead, so that they are

---

[1] 1 Corinthians 2:16.

[2] When our daughter Elsa was eight or nine years old, we lived in La Salle, Colorado, and would often walk through the Colorado country-side perhaps a quarter mile from that stretch of I-25 between Greeley and Denver. During our walk Marcella and I could clearly see the cars and trucks on the freeway and would occasionally comment on them. Elsa would remain silent, until we took her to an oculist who prescribed glasses. With her new glasses an entire new world opened up before her, and for some time she would exclaim, "I can see the cars on the freeway! Look at that bird on the power line," and so on. She had no idea how foggy her eyesight had been, nor did we, until the oculist worked this transformation that corrected the errors in her vision.

without excuse; because that, when they knew God, they glorified him not as God, neither were thankful, but became vain in their imaginations, and their foolish heart was darkened. Professing themselves to be wise, they became fools.[1]

Fortunately, in this confusing picture, there is a way by which we may be assured that we are making progress in coming out of the darkness, or descending deeper into it—even though we may be very immature followers of the Light:

If you are growing in faith and hope and love, *you may know* *that your spiritual vision has been cleared.* If you delight to dwell upon the plan of salvation, upon the glorious manifestations of the divine character, if your heart, in contemplation of the love of God, glows with thankfulness and joy, you may be **sure** that you have been *illuminated* by the beams of the Holy Spirit.[2]

25. ASSURANCE THAT GOD IS TRUE

Trust in [God] at all times, ye people.... Surely men of low degree are vanity, and men of high degree are a lie.... Yea, let God be true, but every man a liar.... God ... cannot lie.[3]

One reason God cannot lie is the fact that if He says something that was not true until He says it, it becomes true as He speaks:

God ... calleth those things which be not as though they were.[4]

He "calleth those things which be not as though they were"; *for when He calls them,* **they are!**[5]

---

[1] Romans 1:20-22.

[2] *Signs of the Times,* 3-27-1893, ¶ 6. Emphases added.

[3] Psalm 62:8, 9; Romans 3:4; Titus 1:2.

[4] Romans 4:17. Italic added.

[5] *Education,* 254. Emphases added.

The rainbow about the throne is an **assurance** that God is true; that in Him is no variableness, neither shadow of turning [James 1:17].[1]

In these times, when truth is regarded as an option in the highest offices of our land, and lies are offered up daily as acceptable fare, Christians are to stand out like those few stars on a tempestuous night, that shine here and there among the clouds[2]—giving a rare, clear testimony in their words and actions for truth and integrity. We should be careful what we say; our words have far-reaching consequences. We can see from the inspired commentary above and from what follows that this is infinitely more so with God.

26. ASSURANCE THAT GOD'S WORD IS TRUE

All scripture is given by inspiration of God.... We have ... a more sure word of prophecy ... knowing ... that no prophecy of the scripture is of any private interpretation.[3]

This scripture given through the apostle may also be rendered: "All scripture is given by inspiration of God.... We have ... a sure word of God ... knowing that no teaching of the scripture is of any prophet's own private interpretation"; that is, we are assured that the Bible says and means what God intends it to say and mean. At the very least this was true at the end of the nineteenth century.

[T]he Lord has preserved this Holy Book by His own miraculous power *in its present* [1888] *shape*—a chart or guidebook to the human family to show them the way to heaven.[4]

---

[1] *Christ's Object Lessons,* 148 (also in *Testimonies for the Church,* VIII, 23).

[2] *Testimonies for the Church,* V, 76.

[3] *2 Timothy* 3:16; 2 Peter 1:19, 20.

[4] *Selected Messages,* I, 15 (Ms 16, 1888, Minneapolis). Italic added.

But although God has made sure "by His ... miraculous power" that the Bible says and means what He intends, even down here at the end of all things earthly, it is oftentimes not clear to the student what that meaning is! For that reason God has provided a reliable Teacher of its true meaning. "Men of God spake as they were moved *by the Holy Ghost.*"[1] God has provided *us* with this same Holy Spirit that moved these men of God in ancient times, to explain to us what He meant for us to understand as that meaning is needed. This divine assistance is provided through several different agencies.

(1) He has promised the "Comforter ... the Spirit of truth," Who "shall teach [us] all things ... whatsoever [Jesus has] said unto [us]."[2] The future tense implies that past understandings will not suffice to meet man's needs in the future as the intensity of the great controversy between Christ and Satan increases.

(2) Through the agency of this Holy Spirit God has provided His people with the comfort, the assurance, of 20 million words (more or less) of reassuring, enlightening counsel, whereby He has opened, illustrated, illuminated, applied, simplified, clarified, and magnified, that challenging volume of His word we call the Bible. This is a fulfilment of a promise, a prophecy, made in the Bible itself:

> [Christ] gave some, apostles; and some, prophets; and some, evangelists; and some, pastors and teachers; for the perfecting of the saints, for the work of the ministry, for the edifying of the body of Christ: till we all come, in the unity of the faith, and of the knowledge of the Son of God, unto a perfect man, *unto the measure of the stature of the fulness of Christ.*[3]

---

[1] 2 Peter 1:21. Italic added.

[2] John 14:16, 17, 26; 16:13.

[3] Ephesians 4:11-13.

112

It seems quite obvious that this promise has not yet reached its fulfilment—Christ's followers do not yet measure up to "the stature of the fulness of Christ"! We can therefore expect those helps mentioned in the promise to still be present in the church as needed. Elsewhere the Bible excludes the desirability of any expansion of the biblical system of truths,[1] but not the further elaboration of those truths which it contains. The Holy Spirit has been promised as an aid to the provision of these further understandings of the Bible system of truths. There is a limited discussion of this work of the Holy Spirit under the topic, "Assurance of Receiving the Holy Spirit," in Chapter 4.

(All uses of italic, except for book and periodical titles, in the following quotations have been supplied by the current writer):

The Scriptures Opened

> This is my work—to *open* the Scriptures to others, as God has opened them to me.[2]

The Scriptures Opened, Illuminated, Applied

> [T]he fact that God has revealed His will to men through His word, has not rendered needless the continued presence and guiding of the Holy Spirit. On the contrary, the Spirit was promised by our Saviour, to *open* the Word to His servants, to *illuminate* and *apply* its teachings. And since it was the Spirit of God that inspired the Bible, it is impossible that the teaching of the Spirit should ever be contrary to that of the Word....

> Through the *illumination* of the Holy Spirit, the scenes of the long-continued conflict between good and evil have been *opened* to the writer of these pages....

---

[1] Revelation 22:18.
[2] *Testimonies for the Church,* VIII, 236.

As the Spirit of God has *opened* to my mind the great truths of His word, and the scenes of the past and the future, I have been bidden to make known to others that which has thus been revealed—to trace the history of the controversy in past ages, and especially ... to shed a light on the fast-approaching struggle of the future....

In these records [of the past] we may see a foreshadowing of the conflict before us. Regarding them in the light of God's word, and by the *illumination* of His Spirit, we may see unveiled the devices of the wicked one, and the dangers which they must shun who would be found "without fault" [Revelation 14:5] before the Lord at His coming.[1]

The Scriptures Simplified

Additional truth is not brought out; but God has through the Testimonies *simplified* the great truths already given.[2]

The Scriptures Made Clearer

Brother J would confuse the mind by seeking to make it appear that the light God has given through the Testimonies is an addition to the word of God; but in this he presents the matter in *a false light.* God has seen fit in this manner to bring the minds of his people to his word, to give them a *clearer* understanding of it.[3]

The Scriptures Magnified

How many have read carefully *Patriarchs and Prophets, The Great Controversy,* and *The Desire of Ages?* I wish all to understand that my confidence in the light that God has given stands firm, because I know that the Holy Spirit's power *magnified* the truth.[4]

(3) Another magnifying glass and illustrator of the word of God may be found in the creation about us.

---

[1] *The Great Controversy* (1911 edition), vii-xi.

[2] *Testimonies for the Church,* II, 605 (Also in V, 665).

[3] *Ibid.,* IV, 246 (Also in V, 663).

[4] *Colporteur Ministry,* 126.

The heavens declare the glory of God and the firmament sheweth his handiwork. Day unto day uttereth speech, and night unto night sheweth knowledge. There is no speech nor language where their voice is not heard.[1]

The wrath of God is revealed from heaven against all ungodliness and unrighteousness of men who hold the truth in unrighteousness because that which may be known of God is manifest to them, for God hath shewed it unto them. For the invisible things of him from the creation of the world are *clearly seen*, being understood by the things that are made, even his eternal power and Godhead; so that they are without excuse.[2]

Doth not even *nature itself* teach you that, if a man have long hair, it is a shame unto him?[3]

In the term "scripture" is included the whole treasure house of revelation and knowledge, in whatever form it is given.[4]

(4)　A fourth means by which God enlightens man's understanding of the Bible is through his own experience.

Those who have felt it necessary to have the students in our schools study many authors are themselves the most ignorant on the great themes of the Bible. The teachers themselves need to take up the Book of all books, and learn from the Scriptures that the gospel has power to prove its own divinity to the humble, contrite mind.[5]

The Bible to me is the voice of God. I have the witness *in myself* that the word of God is true, and that Jesus Christ is the divine Son of God. I am following no cunningly devised fable [2 Peter 1:16].[6]

---

[1] Psalm 19:1-3.

[2] Romans 1:18-20, margin. Italic added.

[3] 1 Corinthians 11:14. Italic added. (It is not the intention of this book's author to here get into the subject of proper personal appearance, but just to show how God uses nature to communicate His will to mankind.)

[4] *Review and Herald,* 8-13-1959, ¶ 10 (First printing of undated manuscript 142).

[5] *Selected Messages,* I, 245 (*The Youth's Instructor,* 10-13-1898).

[6] *Signs of the Times,* 9-3-1894, ¶ 4. Italic added.

And so it is quite evident that God has not only assured us that His word is true, but He has also gone to considerable lengths to further assure us that even after six thousand years of devolution of the human mind resulting from sin, modern man may still clearly understand, through the helps God has provided, what is God's intended meaning of that word, and how it is to be currently applied, so that in times so characterized by innovation and change His people might still have "an anchor of the soul, both sure and steadfast."[1]

It should be mentioned that God's intended meaning of His word may not always be the same as His spokesman's intended meaning, who may not have understood the long-range implications of his messages. The prophets in fact recognized this and searched their own writings, as well as the other scriptures, to discover "what ... the Spirit of Christ which was in them did signify";[2] what did God mean by what He was inspiring them to write or speak? The issue was not what *they* intended to say, but what *God* intended to say. A consequence of this is that, while in seeking the meaning of Bible passages it is helpful to have some understanding of the historical surroundings, of the customs and cultures of the various Bible writers,[3] such knowledge is not as important as some would make it. And the meaning of His word God has assured us may be understood by the commoners of humanity:

> The Bible ... was not written for the scholar alone. On the contrary, *it was designed for the common people,* and the interpretation given by the common people, *when aided by the Holy Spirit,* accords best with the truth as it is in Jesus.[4]

---

[1] Hebrews 6:19.

[2] 1 Peter 1:11.

[3] "Knowledge is power." —*Testimonies for the Church,* IV, 656.

[4] *Testimonies for the Church,* V, 331. Italic added.

The reason the "common people" are assured that the meaning of the Scriptures is directly available to them, without the necessity of human intermediaries, inspiration has clearly stated.

> O my people, they which lead thee cause thee to err.... The leaders of this people cause them to err; and they that are led of them are destroyed.[1]

And so it is well for us to keep in mind that God wishes—through His Spirit—to personally explain His word to us individually, with no other intruding presence, including those identified by inspiration as "scholars." It is in this setting that we have the assurance that a correct understanding of God's word is within our reach.[2]

Caveat emptor!: Of these several methods God has provided to make us knowledgeable in His word, and to make us effective in communicating it, all must be tested against the Bible itself. When doubt arises, the Bible, where it is clear, is the final authority. In opening, illustrating, illuminating, applying, simplifying, clarifying, and magnifying the teachings of the Bible, they must not make the Bible self-contradictory, nor may *any* of these "scriptures" be given a meaning that is internally self-contradictory, or contradictory of any of the others. Where such contradictions arise we can be assured that there are yet flaws in our understanding of the matters at issue.

> "To the law and to the testimony: if they speak not according to this word, it is because there is no light in them" (Isaiah 8:20). Even the work of the Holy Spirit upon the heart is to be tested by the Word of God. The Spirit

---

[1] Isaiah 3:12; 9:16.

[2] Cf. Acts 17:11.

which inspired the Scriptures, always leads to the
Scriptures.[1]

It is clear that the term "Scriptures" in the preceding
reference refers to the more-restricted sense, that is, the
Bible, and does not have the more general meaning given
under (3) above. This is also true of that which immediately
follows below.

> The Holy Scriptures are to be accepted as an authoritative,
> infallible revelation of His will.... Yet the fact that God has
> revealed His will to men through His word, has not
> rendered needless the continued presence and guiding of the
> Holy Spirit.[2]
>
> Let the seeker for truth who accepts the Bible as the in-
> spired word of God, *lay aside every previous idea,* and take
> that Word in its simplicity. He should renounce every sinful
> practice, and enter the Holy of Holies with heart softened
> and subdued, *ready to listen* to what God says.
>
> Do not carry your creed to the Bible, and read the
> Scriptures in the light of that creed.... Let every
> controversy or dispute be settled by "It is written." ...
> Laying aside all creeds or articles prescribed *by any church,*
> we are to read the Bible as the word of God to us.[3]

It is dangerous indeed, but nevertheless quite typical, for us
who belong to the Laodicean era to begin to think that we
understand some concept of the Scriptures, and that we
therefore do not need correction on that "idea." "Thou
sayest, I ... have need of nothing," but are likely to have a
"miserable and ... blind" understanding of that very idea.[4]

---

[1] *Selected Messages,* I, 43 (*General Conference Daily Bulletin,* 4-13-1891).

[2] *The Great Controversy* (1911 edition), vii.

[3] *Review and Herald,* 8-13-1959, ¶ 1-3 (undated Ms 142). Italic added. (Also, in part, in *Our High Calling,* 207.)

[4] Revelation 3:17.

[T]he greatest reason why the people of God are now found in this state of [Laodicean] spiritual blindness, is that they will not receive correction.[1]

We may more safely approach the Scriptures on any subject with the humble attitude that there are likely errors in our thinking on that subject which need to be corrected, and to therefore lay aside our thinking on that subject with the intent of discovering what God's thinking is. Come to the Scriptures, this "Holy of Holies," not seeking support for some idea we may have, but seeking to discover the ideas we should be supporting. If we do this we are assured that we will find the correct ideas we often erroneously think we now have!

> I would impress upon all the fact that a casual reading of the Scriptures is not enough. We must search, and this means the doing of all the word implies.... "If any man willeth to do his will, he shall know of the teaching." John 7:17, Revised Version....
>
> You are not to take your ideas to the Bible, and make your opinions a center around which truth is to revolve. You are to *lay aside your ideas at the door of investigation,* and with humble, subdued hearts, with self hid in Christ, with earnest prayer, you are to seek wisdom from God.... You should desire above all things that you may know the will and ways of the Lord. You should not search for the purpose of finding texts of Scripture that you can construe to prove your theories; for the word of God declares that this is wresting the scriptures to your own destruction [2 Peter 3:16].[2]

---

[1] *Testimonies for the Church,* III, 254f (about 1873).

[2] *Review and Herald,* 9-11-1894, ¶ 2, 3. Italic added.

27. ASSURANCE OF EXPERIENCING THE GLORIES OF HEAVEN

We can apply every positive superlative adjective in human language, plus every desirable quality of which we can think for which no words exist, to the capitol of the universe, called Heaven, and yet fall far short of the reality. We are assured[1] that the mind of man cannot imagine anything as wonderful, beautiful, grand, thrilling, fragrant, tasty, appetizing, soothing, delightful, satisfying, stimulating, rapturous, breath-taking, ecstasy-producing, &c, as the place God has prepared for those who love Him. There are no desirable experiences we have here for which there will not be more desirable and enjoyable, more satisfying experiences in heaven. To say it differently, there are no experiences that we will desire in the future world, no experiences that could make our lives more full and happy that will be missing.

> The treasures of heaven will be opened to supply the wants of every hungering, thirsting soul. All of this character have the **assurance** of one day beholding the glory of that kingdom which as yet the imagination can only faintly grasp.[2]

Delightful sensory, mental, and spiritual perceptions that have been blunted by six thousand years of abuse under sin, and by our own misuse, will by the creative power of God be restored to a level that even exceeds pre-fall, Edenic acuteness; and this will greatly magnify pleasurable sensations of all kinds experienced by the glorified citizens of God's kingdom.

> We shall stand in [God's] presence, and behold the glory of His countenance.... The loves and sympathies which God

---

[1] 1 Corinthians 2:9.

[2] *Signs of the Times*, 2-4-1897, ¶ 5.

Himself has planted in the soul, shall [in Heaven] find truest and sweetest exercise.... There, immortal minds will contemplate with never-failing delight the wonders of creative power, the mysteries of redeeming love.... There the grandest enterprises may be carried forward, the loftiest aspirations reached, the highest ambitions realized; and still there will arise new heights to surmount, new wonders to admire, new truths to comprehend, fresh objects to call forth the powers of mind and soul and body....

With unutterable delight the children of earth enter into the joy and wisdom of unfallen beings.... With undimmed vision they gaze upon the glory of creation—suns and stars and systems, all in their appointed order circling the throne of Deity.... And the years of eternity, as they roll, will bring richer and still more glorious revelations of God and of Christ. As knowledge is progressive, so will love, reverence, and happiness increase....

As Jesus opens before them the riches of redemption, and the amazing achievements in the great controversy with Satan, the hearts of the ransomed thrill with more fervent devotion, and with more rapturous joy they sweep the harps of gold.... One pulse of harmony and gladness beats through the vast creation. From Him who created all, flow life and light and gladness.... From the minutest atom to the greatest world, all things, animate and inanimate, in their unshadowed beauty and perfect joy, declare that God is love.[1]

28. ASSURANCE OF ETERNAL LIFE

Verily, verily, I say unto you, If a man keep my saying, he shall never see death.... He shall never taste of death.[2]

The **assurance** of our Saviour that we may gain the future, immortal life should be sufficient to teach us the importance of following Him here.[3]

---

[1] *The Great Controversy,* 677f.

[2] John 8:51, 52.

[3] *Pacific Union Recorder,* 7-7-1904, ¶ 5.

ASSURANCE OF CLEAR SPIRITUAL INSIGHT

[John 14:1-3 quoted.] This **assurance** of our Saviour should be sufficient to teach us the importance of living the life of Christ in this world, that we may lay hold of the future immortal life.[1]

God does not promise us ease, honor, or wealth in his service, but he **assures** us that all needed blessings will be ours, "with persecutions" [Mark 10:30], and in the world to come "life everlasting" [Luke 18:30].[2]

L ife is very precious to all living creatures; and of all the creatures upon earth, life is especially precious to human beings. They alone have a level of awareness commensurate with the appreciation of the value, the shortness, the Source and fulness of life, and the wonder of eternal life, including our eligibility for it. Life is so dear to us that we will endure great risks, cost, and inconvenience to preserve it, to prolong it—for even a year or two—for ourselves or for those we love; and we feel inexpressible sorrow over the prospect of the loss of it ourselves or over the loss of those dear to us. The newborn Christian enters into a life that measures with the life of God and cannot truly die. He can only experience a temporary sleep, the duration of which seems but an instant.

A dear physician friend of the author lives but a few hundred yards from a busy suburban highway in Southern California. A number of years ago, he was standing outside his home visiting with a neighbor when his daughter, a lovely girl in her mid-teens, left on a date with her boyfriend in his car. Seconds later the father heard the alarming shrieks of rubber on pavement, and a horrific crash. Fearing the worst, he jumped into his car and raced to the scene, to find his daughter fatally injured in the crash. Before she expired in his arms, she weakly cried, "Daddy, I don't want to die."

---

[1] *Signs of the Times*, 7-15-97, ¶ 12.

[2] *Testimonies for the Church*, V, 42 (early 1880s).

Even now as I think of that plaintive cry and the indescribable anguish of father and daughter, it gives me a sinking feeling inside. It seems so final! The very nature of life is that it wishes to continue. What a relief it is when we can assure someone under these terrible circumstances, "It's all right, you'll be alive and well in the morning!" There are circumstances over which we have complete control that make such an assurance fully possible.

God, who made man's emotions with all their inherent liabilities and assets, ranging from uncontrollable grief and fear through perfect peace and ecstatic happiness, has provided the solution for this problem of life. Involved in this solution is the concept of sleep. The Bible often describes as sleep what elsewhere is called death—Job 14:12; Psalm 13:3; Jeremiah 51:39, 57; Matthew 9:24; John 11:11; 1 Corinthians 11:30; 15:51; 1 Thessalonians 4:14, 15; 5:10—for example.

This is not without a reason. Each of us has been practicing for many years the experience of going to sleep without anxiety, with the comfortable assurance that the alarm, a parent, a spouse, perhaps some other friend, the neighbor's rooster, some neurophysiological process, *et cetera.*, will wake us up in the morning. We trust that we will be kept while we sleep, and that we will indeed be awakened when morning comes.

God has provided us with all these thousands of nightly rehearsals so that someday, should time last, when we lay aside our earthly tasks and lie down to sleep we may do so without anxiety, in full assurance that Jesus, who is parent, spouse, friend, and alarm, will call us in the morning; and *this last period of sleep, however long it may be by the clock, will be to the sleeper no longer than any other good night's restful sleep*—but an infinitesimal instant.

He goes to sleep at peace and happy; an instant later, as it were without interruption, he awakens at peace and gloriously happy. How marvelous are God's provisions!

Modern man in an age of surgery "miracles" has other experiences of being put to sleep, or of knowing others who have been put to sleep, and awakened at the will and command of surgeons and anesthesiologists. Their lives are temporarily in the hands of others. It is our privilege, when we go to sleep—die—to have our lives "hid with Christ in God."[1] However, there is an experience from which no one can awaken us, called in the Bible the "second death."[2] It is our privilege through Christ never to become that dead! It was this experience that Jesus was quoted above as saying we need "never taste of."

Every trusting parent, may with complete truthfulness, tell his dying little child, "You're going to sleep now, darlin'; if Jesus comes to visit us tonight; would you like Him to call you in the morning?" And when such a child hears the call of Jesus on resurrection morning and sees her handsome guardian angel towering over her, I can imagine the child's saying to the angel, "Are you Jesus? Last night Daddy told me Jesus might call me this morning." How could one be overwhelmed with uncontrollable grief under such glorious, reassuring circumstances? "I will praise thee, O Lord"; how wonderful are "all thy marvelous works."[3]

> Those who are true to God need not fear the power of men nor the enmity of Satan. In Christ their eternal life is **secure**.[4]

---

[1] Colossians 3:3.

[2] Revelation 2:11; 20:6, 14.

[3] Psalm 9:1.

[4] *The Desire of Ages*, 356.

ASSURANCE OF WHAT?

[Jesus] ascended to the heavenly courts, and from God Himself heard the **assurance** that ... through His blood all might gain eternal life.[1]

Our privileges are far greater than were the privileges of the Jews.... We have had presented to us by the messengers of God the richest feast—the righteousness of Christ, justification by faith, the exceeding great and precious promises of God in his word, free access to the Father by Jesus Christ, the comforts of the Holy Spirit, and the well-grounded **assurance** of eternal life in the kingdom of God.[2]

And there is no reason, none whatsoever, why that life cannot begin right now—today!

The commandment-keeping people of God are to walk in the sunlight of Christ's righteousness, their countenances expressing cheerfulness and thanksgiving, joyful in the **assurance**, "Blessed are they that do his commandments, that they may have right to the tree of life, and may enter in through the gates into the city" [Revelation 22:14].[3]

Our countenances can be so cheerful; we can be possessed with such joyful assurance because we *are* living—*eternally!* From this day forward our cheerfulness and joy need never end. It goes on, and never ends, in Christ. *We* are written there![4]

---

[1] *Ibid.,* 790.

[2] *Review and Herald,* 1-17-1899. ¶ 13.

[3] *Ibid.,* 5-3-1898. ¶ 14.

[4] Cf. Exodus 28:9-21; *Testimonies for the Church,* 251; *Fundamentals of Christian Education,* 273.

Chapter 7

ASSURANCE THAT JESUS MEETS ALL NEEDS

29. ASSURANCE OF SAFETY (SECURITY)

It is guilt that destroys a person's sense of security because he can't escape the never fully absent realization that his future is uncertain, and may be unfavorably decided at any moment. His fearfulness is proportional to his vulnerability. The guilty people's only solution is to surround themselves with walls and bars, armies, firepower, bullet-proof clothing, *et cetera*. In the absence of guilt one is unafraid, because whether his situation is one of illness, old age or other threat of danger, he has the assurance that inside of all the man-made protective devices is a ring of powerful supernatural defenders.[1] His future is in the hands of God, and he views and loves God as his all-wise, all-powerful, ever-present Friend who loves him. Perfect love casts out fear.[2] He does not cling to his present physical life as though it were the only life he would ever have. As he views the unparalleled suffering of God for him he can even rejoice at the prospect of pain and suffering.[3]

---

[1] 2 Kings 6:16, 17.

[2] 1 John 4:18.

[3] Romans 5:1-5.

In Christ the guilty heart has found relief. He is the **sure** foundation. All who make Him their dependence rest in perfect **security**.[1]

The **assurance** that we are under the protection of Omnipotence imparts courage and confidence, inspires a hope that is 'as an anchor of the soul, both sure and steadfast, and which entereth into that within the vail' [Hebrews 6:19]. This **assurance** is a source of strength unknown to the worldling or to the half-hearted professor.[2]

[L]et all realize that they are in peril, and there is no **assurance** of safety except as they comply with the conditions of the text [James 4:7, 8]. The Lord says, "Draw nigh to God." How?—By secret, earnest examination of your own heart; by childlike, heartfelt, humble dependence upon God, making known your weakness to Jesus; and by confessing your sins. Thus you may draw nigh to God, and He will draw nigh to you.[3]

The fact that "the righteousness of Christ; and this alone— *Christ's imputed righteousness*—makes us able to stand against the wiles of the devil"[4] again strongly supports the thesis that the key issue in assurance of security is freedom from guilt.

If we will but keep our eyes fixed on the Saviour, and trust in his power, we shall be filled with a sense of **security**; for the righteousness of Christ will become our righteousness.[5]

While Christians are sleeping at their post, Satan is active, vigilant, and untiring. None are **secure** from his wiles.[6]

The life and words of Christ must be diligently studied, and his instructions cheerfully obeyed. He who will thus gird on the armor of righteousness need not fear the enemies of

---

[1] *The Desire of Ages*, 599.

[2] *Signs of the Times*, 1-28-1886, ¶ 10.

[3] *Youth's Instructor*, 2-8-1894, ¶ 3 (See also *Sons and Daughters of God*, 346).

[4] *Ibid.*, Italic added.

[5] *Review and Herald*, 10-1-1908, ¶ 3.

[6] *Ibid.*, 10-23-1888, ¶ 8 (Minneapolis).

God. He may be **assured** of the presence and protection of the Captain of the Lord's host.[1]

30. ASSURANCE OF FREEDOM FROM FEAR

Closely related to the concept of security is fear of harm—to ourselves, to those dear to us, or to our possessions. The insecure person is a fearful, anxious person. There is a wholesome fear that is "the beginning of wisdom"[2]—reverence for God and the fear of self and sin within, the fear that we will not correctly represent the truth;[3] but the fear experienced by most people—a tormenting fear of trouble—is destructive of mind, soul, and body. This is the fear the men of Saul's army felt when confronted by the half-ton Philistine giant, Goliath. "All the men of Israel, when they saw the man, fled from him, and were sore afraid."[4] This fear tends to produce the very problems of which we are afraid, because "fear hath torment." Unselfish love is healing—because "perfect love casteth out fear."[5] "[Jesus' disciples'] fear in the time of danger revealed their unbelief."[6]

In the section on "Assurance of Security" above, we found that "all who make [Christ] their dependence rest in perfect security." They, like David, know they are surrounded by a wall of heavenly beings that only blessings can penetrate. Because of his dependence upon God, David was no more afraid of Goliath than if confronted by a mouse. To all outward appearances in this "cat and mouse" contest, Goliath was the cat and David the mouse; but David viewed Goliath

---

[1] *Signs of the Times,* 7-21-1881. ¶ 4.

[2] Proverbs 9:10.

[3] *The Great Controversy* (1911 edition). 619.

[4] 1 Samuel 17:24.

[5] 1 John 4:18.

[6] *The Desire of Ages,* 336.

as the mouse and himself as a paw of the Lion of the tribe of Judah.[1] "The righteous are bold as a lion."[2]

> God is our refuge and strength, a very present help in trouble. *Therefore will not we fear,* though the earth be removed, and though the mountains be carried into the midst of the sea; though the waters thereof roar and be troubled, though the mountains shake with the swelling thereof.[3]

It is difficult to imagine a situation more terrifying than that which is described in these verses of the 46th Psalm. If we are unafraid under these circumstances, of what "shall I be afraid?"![4] "Fear in the time of danger" indicates a tenuous, at best, connection with God, and shows that the cords of love that fasten us to Him need to be strengthened.

> God hath not given us the spirit of fear, but of power, and of love, and of a sound mind.[5]

> "God is love." Repeat this sentence whenever temptation presses upon you.[6]

> When the love of God is there ... then you can do anything.[7]

Y ou can do anything"!—you can slay, without fear or trembling, every Goliath-like monster in your path! You can face every fiery furnace, every den of lions, every angry mob. It should be preeminently clear that the love of God is the secret of freedom from fear. Fear (of danger) is a symptom of mental unsoundness, irrationality, separation from God, incipient insanity! It leads to heart

---

[1] Revelation 5:5.

[2] Proverbs 28:1.

[3] Psalm 46:1-3.

[4] Psalm 27:1.

[5] 2 Timothy 1:7.

[6] *Signs of the Times,* 4-9-1894, ¶ 8.

[7] *EGW 1888 Materials,* 159 (Minneapolis, October 1888).

palpitation, unsteadiness of the nerves, serious errors in judgment, and a most miserable existence. But he who is in harmony with, in love with, God, "cannot be made miserable."[1] He will not be afraid though "a thousand shall fall at [his] side, and ten thousand at [his] right hand,"[2] "though the mountains" around him be thrown "into the midst of the sea," and the earth upon which he stands trembles like a leaf.

> The Lord is my light and my salvation; whom shall I fear? The Lord is the strength of my life; of whom shall I be afraid?[3]

> Those who are true to God need not fear the power of men nor the enmity of Satan. In Christ their eternal life is **secure**. Their only fear should be lest they surrender the truth, and thus betray the trust with which God has honored them.[4]

This makes clear that there is a fear that all God's children have and all the world's children lack—fear that they will "surrender the truth." The Bible repeatedly refers to it as the "fear of God," the "fear of the Lord."[5] This fear will remove from us the world's fear of harm and danger! They are mutually exclusive! As one enters, the other leaves. The more we fear God, the less we fear men and devils and their devices.

> As long as you are true to yourself, no adverse power of earth or hell will be able to destroy your peace or interrupt your communion with God. *If you fear God,* you need not walk in **uncertainty**.[6]

---

[1] *Thoughts from the Mount of Blessing,* 28.

[2] Psalm 91:7.

[3] Psalm 27:1.

[4] *The Desire of Ages,* 356.

[5] "Perfecting holiness in the fear of God" (2 Corinthians 7:1); "The fear of the Lord is the beginning of wisdom" (Psalm 111:10; Proverbs 1:7).

[6] *This Day With God,* 334 (To Edson, 11-21-1879). Emphases added.

The life and words of Christ must be diligently studied, and his instructions cheerfully obeyed. He who will thus gird on the armor of righteousness need not fear the enemies of God. He may be **assured** of the presence and protection of the Captain of the Lord's host.[1]

31. ASSURANCE THAT WE WON'T STARVE OR NEED TO BEG

I have been young, and now am old; yet have I not seen the righteous forsaken, nor his seed begging bread.[2]

His place of defence shall be the munitions of the rocks: bread shall be given him; his waters shall be sure.[3]

The assurance that God hears prayer, guarantees that He will hear the prayer of Matthew 6:9-13. Part of that prayer is the request, "Give us this day our daily bread." The meaning of this request is by no means limited to the "staff of life" that appears upon our tables, but it certainly includes that. This gives us the assurance that we need not starve or beg. Even though we have no assurance that the headsman's ax will not fall upon us, or that we will not be burned at the stake, or that we will not die of a lingering disease; and even though we are not promised cake or steak or that we will never go hungry, we *are* promised that our physical necessities for food and water will be supplied to us and to our dependent children.

We close this section by repeating a sentence from the section, "Assurance of Eternal Life," in Chapter 6:

God does not promise us ease, honor, or wealth in his service, but he **assures** us that *all needed blessings* will be

---

[1] *Signs of the Times,* 7-21-1881, ¶ 4.

[2] Psalm 37:25.

[3] Isaiah 33:16.

ours, "with persecutions" [Mark 10:30], and in the world to come "life everlasting" [Luke 18:30].[1]

32. ASSURANCE OF THE DIVINE NATURE

> His divine power hath given unto us all things that pertain unto life and godliness, through the knowledge of him that hath called us to glory and virtue, whereby are given unto us exceeding great and precious promises, that by these ye might be partakers of the divine nature, having escaped the corruption that is in the world through lust.[2]

> Beloved, now are we the sons of God, and it doth not yet appear what we shall be; but we know that, when he shall appear, we shall be like him; for we shall see him as he is.[3]

Partakers of the divine nature, how can it be? It is an incredible thought! What can man's destiny be? Would the spotless God of heaven allow dust in the supreme councils of the universe? It is already there. Then, you say, someone needs to bring in a dust-cloth, the "dirt brush." But who in the universe would give God's only-begotten-Son the dust off! "He knoweth our frame; he remembereth that we are dust" (Psalm 103:14); and His Son, the Son of Man, got that same frame from Mary and all her ancestors, and now carries it into the inner throne-room of the universe. Christ in us assures us that we may be partakers of His nature; we in Him is our assurance that it is our privilege to be with Him wherever He is.

> They all may be one; as thou, Father, art in me, and I in thee; ... they also may be one in us.... Father, I will that they also, whom thou hast given me, be *with me where I am*.[4]

---

[1] *Testimonies for the Church.* V. 42. Italic added.

[2] 2 Peter 1:3, 4.

[3] 1 John 3:2.

[4] John 17:21, 24. Italic added.

> Put on the new man, which *after God* is created in righteousness and true holiness.[1]

> Therefore if any man be in Christ, he is a new creature; old things are passed away; behold, all things are become new.[2]

Man is inestimably privileged to receive here and now a new nature, to become a new creation of God, a partaker of the divine nature, designed "after God"—to be like God. When this happens, we are enabled to bring great hope and assurance where there was little or none. Having received this new spirit man will later receive an immortal, incorruptible, glorified body. Job referred to this body many centuries before Jesus was born in Bethlehem when he said: "And though ... worms destroy this [corruptible] body, yet in my [incorruptible] flesh shall I see God."[3]

> [Christ] desires that we shall abide in Him, that He may work through us in keeping before the world such a representation of the infinite love of God as He Himself gave. Through *our lives* the despondent may receive an **assurance** that it is possible to be partakers of the divine nature, and by taking hold of this divinity win the victory that all must win who shall enter in through the gates into the city.[4]

I have an extensive commentary of nearly two hundred testimonies of the Holy Spirit discussing the what, how, results, and other ramifications of receiving the divine nature; but our brief treatment here is intended to focus on the *assurance* that we can have this unimaginable experience, whatever that glorious experience is.

---

[1] Ephesians 4:24. Italic added.

[2] 2 Corinthians 5:17.

[3] Job 19:26.

[4] *Sermons and Talks*, II, 294. Italic added.

33. ASSURANCE OF HAPPINESS

A brief inspection of the topic, "Assurance of Love," in Chapter 2 should quickly convince the reader that an intimate love relationship with God through His Son, the man Christ Jesus, is the Christian's greatest source of unalloyed and ever increasing happiness and thrills. The remarkable consequences of such a relationship are further expanded under the topic, "Assurance of an Intimately Present, Abiding Christ," also in Chapter 2.

> These things have I spoken unto you, that my joy might remain in you, and that your joy might be full.[1]

> Why should not our joy be full—full, lacking nothing? We have an **assurance** that Jesus is our Saviour, and that we may draw freely from Him. We may partake freely of the rich provision that He has made for us in His Word. We may take Him at His word, believe on Him, and know that He will give us grace and power to do just as He bids us. He has given us every **assurance**, and He will fulfill all that He has promised.[2]

It would be puzzling if, with the dozens of assurances listed and to some extent, discussed, so far, that the true Christian should have bouts of unhappiness, of moodiness and gloom. Though there is much to cause him concern and sorrow—the sorrowful sufferings of our Lord (to insure the happiness of His followers!), the incredible inhumanity of man to his fellow man,[3] the trashing of God's creation, &c ad infinitum—in all his sorrow it is his privilege to "rejoice ... *always*."[4] "*Nothing* can make them sad, when Jesus makes them glad with His presence";[5] and "Who shall separate us

---

[1] John 15:11.

[2] *Sermons and Talks*, II, 293 (3-10-1908).

[3] "The inhumanity of man toward man is our greatest sin" —*The Ministry of Healing*, 163.

[4] Philippians 4:4.

[5] *The Desire of Ages*, 331.

from ... Christ?"[1] "Can the children of the bride-chamber mourn as long as the bridegroom is *with* them?"[2]

> God is the eternal, uncreated Fountain of all good. All who trust in him will find him to be this. To those who serve him, looking to him as their Heavenly Father, he gives the **assurance** that he will fulfill his promises. His joy will be in their hearts, and their joy will be full.[3]

> [The cross] is the **assurance** to us that our joy may be full.[4]

The greatest love that could possibly be manifested in the universe is testified to by the most supreme suffering. There is no mystery there; we see representations (inadequate, to be sure) of such love often in the suffering that mothers of many kinds of creatures are willing to bear that their offspring may survive.[5] Those of us who are adults are aware of how we are drawn to our mothers by their toil-worn hands. What *is* most mysterious is that the reminders of this suffering—the scars of the wounds in Christ's head and side and hands and feet should be our light of eternal assurance, not of dark sorrow, but of the brightness of joy.[6] There will be no memory of the suffering sinners have born, only these reminders in our Saviour of His sorrow and suffering—and this will only increase the joy of the saved! However, the joy

---

[1] Romans 8:35.

[2] Matthew 9:15. Italic added.

[3] *Review and Herald*, 5-5-1910, ¶ 8.

[4] *Signs of the Times*, 4-11-1892, ¶ 11.

[5] Along with several others, I once witnessed a heroic episode of mother love in the form of a cottontail rabbit who had a nest of baby bunnies in a small pile of hay. While we were near her nest she stayed nearby. Then a most touching scene occurred when a large gopher snake, fully capable of swallowing the newborns, began to approach her nest. Normally she would have fled before such a formidable foe, but not under these circumstances. She charged the snake grabbing its midsection in her teeth and shaking it. The snake attacked her, repeatedly striking her nose until it was quite bloodied; but she did not give up the battle until she had driven the intruder into a section of two-inch pipe which we then removed from the scene. She then began to attend to her bloodied nose and the objects of her mother love.

[6] "One reminder alone [of sin] remains: our Redeemer will ever bear the marks of His crucifixion. Upon His wounded head, upon His side, His hands and feet, are the only traces of the cruel work that sin has wrought.... 'He had bright beams coming out of his side: and there was the hiding of his power' [Habakkuk 3:4 (margin)]." —*The Great Controversy* (1911 edition), 674.

will not be in His suffering, but in the love that this suffering reveals:

> [God's children] find greatest joy *in the **assurance** of his great love* wherewith he has loved us.[1]

> "He that believeth on me, the works that I do shall he do also.... And whatsoever ye shall ask in my name, that will I do.... If ye shall ask anything in my name, I will do it" [John 14:12-14]. The faith here brought to view is not a casual faith; it is a living, earnest, active faith, that takes God at his word, and relies upon his pledged promises. This faith brings peace, and constitutes the children of God the light of the world. They live in the bright beams of the Sun of Righteousness. It is enough to make the soul joyful to have such **assurances**—a Comforter always with us, and we revealing to the world in hopefulness, in joyfulness, that we have been called out of darkness into his marvelous light.[2]

34. ASSURANCE OF CONDEMNATION

A ssurance of condemnation? Surely not! What a most unwelcome surprise! What assurance can there be in condemnation? Negatively speaking, we can certainly say that under certain conditions, of which we are not left in doubt, we will *assuredly* be condemned, as the following counsel affirms:

> There are many now who entertain the same feeling of self-congratulation that the Pharisee had [Luke 18:11]. Does this feeling rise in your heart in any degree?... If so, you may be **assured** that while you commend yourself, the condemnation of God rests upon you. You may be thought excellent in character. Your name may be registered on the church-book; but it is not written in the Lamb's book of life.[3]

---

[1] *Signs of the Times*, 4-11-1895. ¶ 5.

[2] *Ibid.*, 12-7-1891. ¶ 1.

[3] *Ibid.*, 2-19-1885. ¶ 9.

That is a terribly dark pronouncement. However, there is a positive side to this. God's assurance that He will prompt us with a guilty conscience, with convictions of condemnation if we turn, perhaps unknowingly to ourselves, from righteousness to unrighteousness, is among our great blessings—one of those divine provisions to prevent us from plunging into an approaching crevasse. The (at times unwelcome) awareness that we are heading in a wrong and dangerous direction may, at our peril, be ignored and bludgeoned into silence; but it will re-awaken, perhaps too late to prevent the plunge. But be thankful that because of it we may escape the abyss.

There is an angel at my side who will tap me on the shoulder and whisper in my ear when God detects that I am about to make a wrong turn. It is wonderfully reassuring to know that we may have the privilege of being convicted of wrong *before* the wrong is done—even unconsciously. The author has experienced many times the prompting of heavenly beings to a better course of action when he was about to say or do something which would not serve God's purposes properly. And with growth in grace, sharper ears detect these promptings more frequently and selectively. You may have had similar experiences.

> [A]ngels are appointed to watch over us, and if we put ourselves under their guardianship, then in every time of danger they will be at our right hand. When unconsciously we are in danger of exerting a wrong influence, the angels will be by our side prompting us to a better course, choosing our words for us, and influencing our actions.[1]

My wife Marcella's Mother, Enid, a daughter of Elder and Mrs. W. C. Hankins who spent twenty years in Amoy, China, was born and reared in Amoy. The Chinese dialect,

---

[1] *Christ's Object Lessons,* 341f.

Amoyese, was Enid's first language, since her playmates were Chinese and the Hankins were committed to using only Amoyese about the house in an effort to become more proficient themselves in this difficult Chinese dialect. The Hankinses eventually returned from Amoy, Enid married, and Marcella was born. Marcella's mother, Enid, because of her upbringing in a Chinese culture, would often use Chinese expressions about the house. Marcella picked up a number of these, even though she has never been to China. These expressions turn out to be quite convenient at times if one wishes to communicate something without being understood by others nearby. One such expression is phonetically something like "Mm dahng Kahng," which is a caution to stop saying something. I have heard it numerous times!

On one such occasion I was conducting a study in a Baptist prayer meeting when Marcella could see I was heading in a direction likely to leave a wrong impression on the audience. Suddenly I heard a voice coming softly but clearly from the middle of the congregation, "Mm dahng kahng." I responded to this "tap on the shoulder" from my angel wife, and changed direction in midstream, somewhat to the surprise of the mystified listeners, but to the benefit of all. God has many ways to use his messengers to guide us if we are appreciative of this help. It is a wonderful assurance for defective humanity to know that they can have such help and be saved from making mistakes that might lead astray those under their influence.

35. ASSURANCE OF THE ORDERLY FULFILMENT OF GOD'S WORD

We may be assured that God's plans, as revealed in His Word, will be fulfilled in their proper time and order. His "purposes know no haste and no delay."[1]

> The history which the great I AM has marked out in His word, uniting link after link in the prophetic chain, from eternity in the past to eternity in the future, tells us where we are today in the procession of the ages, and what may be expected in the time to come. All that prophecy has foretold as coming to pass, until the present time, has been traced on the pages of history, and we may be **assured** that all which is yet to come will be fulfilled in its order.[2]

36. ASSURANCE OF ASSURANCES

Of whatever God has taken the pains to assure us we may be sure will be carried out, if we meet the conditions that His grace has made quite possible. He has assured us that all of these 36 interrelated assurances may be a part of our experience as we journey heavenward. This in itself is a most wonderful assurance.

> We may all rest in the **assurance** that whatever the love of God has devised in man's behalf will be executed. Justice and judgment are the habitation of His throne; mercy and truth go before His face. In the cross of Christ mercy and truth met together; righteousness and peace kissed each other.[3]

Marvelous assurance!

---

[1] *The Desire of Ages,* 32.

[2] *Education,* 178.

[3] *Signs of the Times,* 4-7-1898, ¶ 9.

PART TWO

ASSURANCE—
THE WHERE
AND HOW OF IT

Chapter 8

ASSURANCE—<u>WHERE</u> IS IT FOUND?

If a person who had struggled many years seeking to just keep food on the table should be notified that he had inherited a handsome estate from a deceased distant relative but received no instruction as to where to go to claim his good fortune, the knowledge of this improved status would do little but add to the frustrations of an already difficult existence. God has not only revealed how fortunate we are as a result of His immense love and generosity, but has, in explicit detail, provided careful instructions concerning the where and how of beginning immediately to profit from this great beneficence. The subject of this chapter involves taking a look at what God has said concerning *where* we may find these blessings that have so much to do with our walking through this dangerous world fearlessly and with perfect assurance of all those 36 blessings of which we are assured and are discussed in the first seven chapters of this book. Let us begin at the beginning.

1. ASSURANCE IS FOUND IN JESUS

All justified assurance is found in Christ. All else is an illusory counterfeit, of varying degrees of deceitfulness. We have repeated here a sample, with very little context, of that counsel that specifically refers to our Saviour as the Source of assurance. The interested student may find much more that, for various reasons, is not included here.

> It was Christ who from the bush on Mount Horeb spoke to Moses saying, "I AM THAT I AM.... I AM hath sent me unto you." Exodus 3:14. This was the pledge of Israel's deliverance. So when He came "in the likeness of men" [Philippians 2:7], He declared Himself the I AM.... "I AM the Good Shepherd." "I AM the living Bread." "I AM the Way, the Truth, and the Life." John 10:11; 6:51; 14:6.... I AM the **assurance** of every promise. I AM; be not afraid. "God with us" [Matthew 1:23] is the **surety**[1] of our deliverance from sin, the **assurance** of our power to obey the law of heaven.[2]

The Bible offers several representations of the true church. One of these is a building with a stone foundation—"the apostles and prophets," all tied into a "chief corner stone," Jesus Christ—in which the church members are described as living stones in the superstructure resting upon the foundational messages of the apostles and prophets, and through them, upon Jesus.[3] This metaphorical structure provides the framework for the concept of the believer's assurance in Christ.

> When we individually rest upon Christ, with **full assurance of faith**, trusting alone to the efficacy of his blood to cleanse from all sin, we shall have peace in believing that what God has promised he is able to perform.[4]

An ever-present danger to the security of the Christian is that he will step off the true foundation and begin to think and act as if he and others can build upon *his* accomplishments instead of those of Christ. In the Bible such a structure is said to be of "wood, hay, stubble," and will not pass the test of fire.[5] However it is possible to build an enduring

---

[1] A "surety" is something that "gives assurance" —Webster.

[2] *The Desire of Ages*, 24. Capitalization in the original.

[3] Ephesians 2:20, 21; 1 Peter 2:5, 6; 1 Corinthians 3:10-17.

[4] *Review and Herald*, 3-5-1889, ¶ 5 (South Lancaster, 1-1889).

[5] 1 Corinthians 3:11-14.

structure, characterized as "gold, silver, precious stones." He who builds such a structure "shall receive a reward." One component of the reward is the ability to walk through this dangerous world of floods, mud slides, earthquakes, fires, tornadoes, hurricanes, power struggles (and outages), crime, war (with weapons of mass destruction), sickness, *et cetera*, without fear. God's foundation "standeth sure," and we are assured that "underneath are the everlasting arms."[1]

> God is our refuge and strength, a very present help in trouble. Therefore will not we fear, though the earth be removed, and though the mountains be carried into the midst of the sea.... Be still and know that I am God.[2]

> Those who fail to realize their constant dependence upon God will be overcome by temptation. We may now *suppose* that our feet stand **secure**, and that we shall never be moved. We may say with confidence, I know in whom I have believed; nothing can shake my faith in God and in His word.... [But] only through realizing our own weakness and looking steadfastly unto Jesus can we walk **securely**.[3]

The solution to our anxieties, fears, and uncertainties is to direct our eyes to Jesus. As we do this we will find that He is returning our gaze. When two people are falling in love and their eyes lock together, things happen. The pulse and respiration accelerate. A feeling of breathlessness and weakness and the desire to surrender are almost overwhelming. So it is when one beholds Jesus face to face by faith. The strength of the attraction is awesome. "*Behold* what ... love the Father hath bestowed upon us."[4] As we behold Jesus beholding us and our eyes of faith lock onto His, miracles happen. The experience is sometimes so powerful, the connection so strong, the voltage so high, that

---

[1] 2 Timothy 2:19; Deuteronomy 33:27.

[2] Psalm 46:1, 2, 10.

[3] *The Desire of Ages*, 382. Italic added.

[4] 1 John 3:1.

one may be prostrated on the floor. Confidence goes off the chart, uncertainties vanish, the weak become "as David."[1] Assurance spurts upward. Those half-ton Goliaths in our path fall headlong to the earth.

> We may take life's controversies and troubles to his feet; for he loves us. His every word and look invite our **confidence**.[2]

> If we will but keep our eyes fixed on the Saviour, and trust in his power, we shall be filled with a sense of **security**; for the righteousness of Christ will become our righteousness.[3]

> I point you to the cross of Calvary. The cross is everything to us.... It is to be our support in every trial, our refuge in every sorrow. It is the **assurance** to us that the Father loves us, and has given his Son for us. It is the **assurance** to us that our joy may be full.[4]

2. ASSURANCE IS FOUND IN GOD'S LOVE AND POWER

> When we were yet without strength ... Christ died for the ungodly.... God commendeth his love toward us in that while we were yet sinners, Christ died for us.[5]

It is a wonderful experience to be loved, disinterestedly—that is, by someone who has no self-interest, who makes no demand of payment in return; and that is fortunate for us, for we have nothing to pay! Such selfless love inspires faith; and love for such a person follows. Thus love begets love.[6] Whoever you are, you do not need to feel that "nobody loves me," for someone does love you, someone more engaging

---

[1] Zechariah 12:8.

[2] *Review and Herald,* 10-30-1900, ¶ 12.

[3] *Ibid.,* 10-1-1908, ¶ 3.

[4] *Signs of the Times,* 4-11-1892, ¶ 11.

[5] Romans 5:6, 8.

[6] "Love begets love, affection begets affection" (*Testimonies for the Church,* II, 95). "Genuine faith is followed by love" (*Ibid.,* V, 219). "The gold mentioned by Christ, the True Witness [Revelation 3:18], which all must have, has been shown me to be faith and love combined, and love takes the precedence of faith" (*Ibid.,* II, 30).

than the most wonderful friend, the most likeable Prince Charming you could imagine. All may be fully assured that God loves them and that at least one other human being does also—the Son of Man, Christ Jesus.

> He would have His servants bear testimony to the fact that through His grace men ... may rejoice in the **assurance** of His great love.[1]

> In times of sudden difficulty or peril, the heart may send up its cry for help to One who has pledged Himself to come to the aid of His faithful, believing ones whenever they call upon Him. In every circumstance, under every condition, the soul weighed down with grief and care, or fiercely assailed by temptation, may find **assurance**, support, and succor in the unfailing love and power of a covenant-keeping God.[2]

God loves us enough to marry us, and He will be faithful to the marriage vow (not by stern resolve but because His love is everlasting, never failing[3]). His *desire* is to be close to us, to keep us close to Him. "With lovingkindness have I *drawn* thee" (close to me). He assures us, "My covenant will I not break," and affirms, "I am married unto you."[4]   There are therefore *no spouseless parents—or companionless persons!* "God shall supply *all* your need ... by Christ Jesus."[5] Now if God has supplied "all" our needs—*all!*—what *need* can we have that is left unsupplied?! What an assurance!

No one is condemned to the single state! But, you object, I need *human* companionship. Truly spoken—"It is not good" for man (or woman) to "be alone"[6]; and that is precisely what

---

[1] *The Desire of Ages*, 826.

[2] *Prophets and Kings*, 631, 632.

[3] Jeremiah 31:3.

[4] Psalm 89:34; Jeremiah 3:14.

[5] Philippians 4:19. Italic added.

[6] Genesis 2:18.

the incarnation provides, the most excellent human companionship one could hope for or desire! The *human being,* Christ Jesus, will not say "No" to your proposal for companionship or marriage, nor will He ever divorce you— but you are free to divorce Him. You can be the most intimate partners—forever! There is no need for anyone to ever be lonely. Was John lonely on Patmos? No, because *he was not alone!* He did not ask human companionship. Jesus had already provided that.[1] Is this not one reason why Jesus says, "They which shall ... obtain that [future] world ... neither marry, nor are given in marriage"?[2]

A result of the plan of redemption and incarnation is that it has become possible for us to be closer to God than even the sinless Adam and Eve in the Garden of Eden. Sin produced such a separation between man and his Creator[3] that they were, in effect, divorced. Furthermore conflict and competition were introduced into the marriage relation, so that in many cases the relationship became more like hell than heaven. But now, through redemption, they are reunited in a way that enables them to be closer than ever—God has become one of us! He has mysteriously created a finite, everlasting, human version of Himself so that it is possible for Him to be close to us in the most understanding, intimate, satisfying, human way.

The love of God, how measureless, how powerful, how impossible to plumb its depths! We will have, for all eternity, this most pleasant task of seeking to comprehend its

---

[1] Rather strong assertions have been made in the paragraphs above about the *possibility* of our being free from aloneness in this world, no matter what is the current status of our relationship to the rest of humankind upon this planet. However, we must not ignore the fact that a first step God often uses in bringing a lonely person to an understanding of the sufficiency of the companionship of the human being, Jesus, is to find him true friends among Jesus' spiritual siblings, His brethren and sisters. And—we might add—one of the best cures for loneliness is to get involved in resolving someone else's need for a true friend.

[2] Luke 20:35.

[3] Isaiah 59:2.

fullness, always finding that there is yet a still more satisfying experience within reach beyond. Through the entire span of infinite time we will have the privilege of drawing, and being drawn, closer to God by His love and power, as manifested through the incarnation of His only-begotten Son.

And we, being drawn ever closer to God, will ever be drawn closer to one another. It will be a grand never-ending, ever-increasing fellowship of love—love received and love bestowed. What a life! What assurance!

When two are falling in love, their desires are that they can spend more and more time in closer and closer proximity; and their activities are arranged to satisfy this mutual interest until their plans and desires are finally consummated in the closeness of the marriage relation. An important difference between our union with God and this human figure is that we will *forever* continue to find ways, previously unknown to us, by which our relationship to God and to each other may grow closer—closer than anything we could possibly know in our present mortal state.

What a future! It sends me into spine-tingling ecstasy just writing about it! Continuing with the marriage metaphor, Hosea writes about this closeness as follows—in the context of reclaiming a wandering spouse from the lowest depths:

> I will betroth thee unto me *forever;* yea, I will betroth thee unto me in righteousness and in judgment, and in lovingkindness, and in mercies. I will even betroth thee unto me in faithfulness; and thou shalt know the Lord.[1]

Notice the final clause—"Thou shalt know the Lord." When sin first entered it was necessary for man, having chosen to divorce God and marry another, to be expelled from the

---

[1] Hosea 2:19, 20.

Garden of Eden and its tree of life lest the sinful divorcee enter the precincts of the Godhead, man's original high destiny.

> The Lord God said, Behold, the man is become *as one of us,* to know good and evil: and now, lest he put forth his hand, and take also of the tree of life, and eat, and live forever; therefore the Lord God sent him forth from the garden of Eden, to till the ground from whence he was taken. So he drove out the man; and he placed at the east of the garden of Eden Cherubims [sic], and a flaming sword which turned every way, to keep the way of the tree of life.[1]

Adam and Eve had chosen to separate themselves from the ways of God and to form an adulterous relationship with the Serpent, Satan. God gave them their choice; but this choice was an unwitting one. They did not yet *know* the depths of the love of God, nor the depths of the malignity of Satan. The solution to this separation that iniquity produced between man and God[2] is to educate him to the intent of clearing up this misunderstanding of those two facts—the love of God and the deceptive evil that is Satan. "This is life eternal that they might *know* thee, the only true God."[3] Jesus Christ is the medium through which such a knowledge—of the true and counterfeit husbands—has been conveyed. This knowledge is what Hosea has written about above.

> To know God is to love Him.[4]

> Now shall the prince of this world [Satan] be cast out. And I, if I be lifted up from the earth, will *draw all* ... unto me.[5]

Jesus was a walking revelation of love throughout His years on earth. Then as He was "lifted up from the earth" by the

---

[1] Genesis 3:22-24.

[2] Isaiah 59:2.

[3] John 17:3.

[4] *The Desire of Ages,* 22.

[5] John 12:31, 32. Italic added.

malignity of the serpent,[1] Satan's character of hate and God's character of love were so fully revealed, that any sympathy for Satan was forever removed from the hearts of *"all"* the created beings in the universe. By this one act of the incarnation, life, crucifixion, resurrection, and current ministry in heaven of the Only-begotten Son of God we are fully assured that sin and sinning will come to "an utter end; affliction shall not rise up the second time."[2]

This is why there is so much power in the scriptures [taken in the general sense given in the last paragraph of (3), Section 26, Chapter 6]. These revelations of the love, the justice, the reasonableness of God, as explained to us by the witness of the Holy Spirit, will so fully remove from us all doubts about God that never again will we find the possibility within ourselves to turn against Him. The very idea, as personalized by Satan, will be abhorrent to all created beings including humanity when once they understand what actually happened, and become in spirit a part of the heavenly world.

> His hatred, carried out in the death of the Son of God, placed Satan where his true diabolical character was revealed to all created intelligences that had not fallen through sin.... Every sentiment of sympathy or pity which [angels] had ever felt for Satan in his exile, was quenched in their hearts.... [I]t caused the angels to shudder with horror, and severed forever the last tie of sympathy existing between Satan and the heavenly world.[3]

> In every circumstance, under every condition, the soul weighed down with grief and care, or fiercely assailed by temptation, may find **assurance**, support, and succor in the unfailing love and power of a *covenant-keeping* God.[4]

---

[1] Numbers 21:9; John 3:14.

[2] Nahum 1:9.

[3] *The Spirit of Prophecy*, III, 183, 184.

[4] *Prophets and Kings*, 632. Italic added.

During a two-week series of meetings by A. T. Jones and E. G. White in Chicago during late March and early April of 1889, a sequel to the Minneapolis meetings of 1888 notoriety, the Lord's messenger made some comments pertinent to the subject of assurance before us:

> Their prayers now [after a week of meetings] are filled with earnest, simple faith that takes God at His word. All now seem to have warm hearts. The love of Christ is **assurance** to them of their acceptance, and they long to speak and acknowledge the great goodness of God in providing them a righteousness which is pure, spotless, efficacious. —*The EGW 1888 Materials,* 283 (Chicago, 4-7-89).

3. ASSURANCE IS FOUND IN GOD'S WORD ASSOCIATED WITH CHEERFUL, SELFLESS OBEDIENCE

Take the word of Christ as your **assurance**.[1]

Men are inclined to surround themselves with all the protection they can afford. The nature of these efforts often provides eloquent testimony as to the source of men's assurance of safety. These devices include walls equipped to detect trespassers, window bars, armed guards, sophisticated weaponry and electronic alarm devices, secret escape routes, dogs (and other animals), armies, &c. Great effort is expended to learn methods of self-defense and of how to incapacitate an attacker. But these methods alone can never provide true assurance of security. The apprehension of Elisha's servant in the presence of an unfriendly environment provides an example of the result of relying upon human devices alone for security. The enemy can always invent an attack plan or device capable of abridging any man-made defense. The prophet himself reveals a safer method. The account is given in the sixth chapter of the second book of Kings.

---

[1] *Christ's Object Lessons,* 146.

When Elisha's servant awakened in Dothan on a certain morning and discovered the city to be surrounded with a "great host" of hostile Syrian warriors, all armed to the teeth with the latest weapons of destruction, in anxious fear he cried out, "Alas! ... how shall we do?"[1] This is the spirit of those who have placed their assurance in human devices alone. Elisha's unperturbed response is a jewel: "Fear not, for they that be with us are more than they that be with them." This is the reaction that every man or woman, clad in the armory of heaven and surrounded with its armies, can give to every person regardless of how outgunned to human eyesight they may appear to be at the moment.

> All [Jesus'] words are spirit and life [John 6:63]. Accepted and obeyed, they will give peace and happiness and **assurance** forever [Isaiah 32:17].[2]

"Forever" suggests that there need never be a time when we have any necessity to be anxious or lacking in peace of mind and soul.

> The Comforter is given that he may take of the things of Christ and show them unto us, that he may present in their rich **assurance** the words that fell from his lips, and convey them with living power to the soul who is obedient, who is emptied of self.[3]

The weapon we wield to slay the giants confronting us is not David's sling, but the two-edged sword of the Spirit, the unconquerable Word of God, an anvil that has worn out many hammers, the Word that was made flesh and dwelt among us.[4] With this weapon in our grasp, our hand is steady, our nerves calm, and our eyes true as we face down a predacious enemy stalking the land with cutting-edge

---

[1] 2 Kings 6:15.

[2] *Review and Herald.* 4-12-1892. ¶ 19.

[3] *Signs of the Times.* 12-25-1893. ¶ 5.

[4] John 1:14. Cf. Ephesians 6:10-17.

weapons of mass destruction, breathing flame and threatenings, seeking whom he may devour.[1]

> One sentence of Scripture is of more value than ten thousand of man's ideas or arguments.... [W]hen we submit to God's way, the Lord Jesus guides our minds and fills our lips with **assurance**.[2]

Through the assurances of the Word of God and the witness within of the Spirit of that Word that we belong to the family of God, calm descends upon every inward uprising, upon every unsettling experience of the human heart.

> We have most precious promises in the word of God, which ought to give us courage and confidence. They should enable us to come out of **uncertainty** and darkness, to come where we may know that the Spirit beareth witness with our spirit that we are the children of God [Romans 8:16].[3]

> [T]he words and promises of Christ are our **assurance**. On these we must rely, and reveal Christ to our world.[4]

> The **assurance** is in God's word. God has said, and it will be done....

> We must hold fast the promises.... [T]hese are our **assurances**.[5]

> [I]n ["the Word of God"] we are to find our **assurance**.[6]

> In perfect obedience to [God's] holy will, we are to manifest adoration, love, cheerfulness, and praise, and thus honor and glorify God. It is in this way alone that man may reveal the character of God in Christ to the world, and make manifest

---

[1] 1 Peter 5:8.

[2] *Testimonies for the Church*, VII, 71.

[3] *Signs of the Times*, 11-1-1889, ¶ 1.

[4] *Ibid.*, 11-30-1891, ¶ 6.

[5] *Review and Herald*, 4-12-1887, ¶ 8.

[6] *Signs of the Times*, 12-3-1894, ¶ 3.

to men that happiness, peace, **assurance**, and grace come from obedience to the law of God.[1]

Those who do accept the evidences of God's word will have an experience that will be as a barrier against infidelity, for they will be *translated* out of darkness into the precious light of faith, hope, and **assurance**.[2]

Have not the precious words spoken by Christ, the Prince of God, an **assurance** and power that should have great influence upon us, that our heavenly Father is more willing to give the Holy Spirit to them that ask Him than parents are to give good gifts to their children? [Luke 11:13].[3]

4. ASSURANCE IS FOUND IN THE MINISTRY OF THE HOLY SPIRIT

The Holy Spirit is the key player in every aspect of assurance. This is the gift of all gifts that Christ left us when He returned to heaven forty days after His resurrection. The Spirit is the One called to our side to replace Christ who would find it necessary to be physically far away. The plan of redemption called for Him to retain the position restrictive results of His incarnation into eternity. His humanity is such an encumbrance as to be incompatible with the divine property of omnipresence. Jesus paid the high price of *eternally* sacrificing this aspect of divinity in order to bring humanity into a closer relationship with God than had previously been possible for created beings. [4]

But we are assured that the Spirit is such a perfect representative of Jesus that it is just as if Jesus were ever present on earth by the side of each of earth's billions of

---

[1] *Review and Herald,* 3-9-1897, ¶ 6.

[2] *Ibid.,* 9-3-1894, ¶ 4. Italic added.

[3] *Selected Messages,* II, 243 (Letter 7, 1892).

[4] "Cumbered with humanity, Christ could not be in every place personally. Therefore it was for [His followers'] interest that He should go to the Father, and send the Spirit to be His successor on earth.... By His Spirit the Saviour would be accessible to all." —*The Desire of Ages,* 669.

men, women and children. Only through this gift of the Spirit can we receive any other blessing, because all gifts come by grace through Christ.[1] He comes with a full chest of tools in the Scriptures, and in all the lessons of the natural universe about us (in this consider the possible implications of a broader meaning of the term, "scriptures"[2]). The brief treatment of this subject here is not designed to be a measure of its importance, but because the topic is so large and important that many books have been devoted to this topic alone. It is a desire of the author that this book be kept short!

> The Comforter is given that he may take of the things of Christ and show them unto us, that he may present in their rich **assurance** the words that fell from his lips, and convey them with living power to the soul who is obedient, who is emptied of self.[3]

5. WHERE <u>NOT</u> TO LOOK FOR ASSURANCE

> The people are fast being lulled to a **fatal security**, to be awakened only by the outpouring of the wrath of God.[4]

We cannot expect to find assurance in self-merit (no matter how talented we may be), in feelings of well-being, or in other human beings, whatever their capacity.

> I have listened to testimonies like this: "I have not the light that I desire; I have not the **assurance** of the favor of God."
> ... Are you expecting that your merit will recommend you to the favor of God, and that you must be free from sin before you trust his power to save?[5]

---

[1] "[T]he Holy Spirit ... would bring in its train all other blessings." —*Signs of the Times,* 4-3-1893, ¶ 3.

[2] "In the term 'scripture' is included the whole treasure house of revelation and knowledge, in whatever form it is given." —*Review and Herald,* 8-13-1959 (This manuscript, written prior to 1916, was first printed in 1959). For additional discussion of the scope of meaning of the term "scripture" see the introductory remarks for chapter 1, and the sub-topics in chapter 1—"Assurance of receiving the Holy Spirit" and "Assurance That God's Word Is True."

[3] *Signs of the Times,* 12-25-1893, ¶ 5.

[4] *The Great Controversy* (1911 edition), 562.

[5] *Review and Herald,* 4-22-1884, ¶ 5.

We are to find the **assurance** of our acceptance with God in his written promise, not in a happy flight of *feeling*.[1]

Where we look for assurance has much to do with the effectiveness of our witnessing. Where there is a heavy emphasis on feeling, we cannot lead others to a proper faith, to childlike trust in God. Working with Christ for the lost, however, is clearly not a feelingless experience. At times, during witnessing experiences, those laboring together with God have even been prostrated upon the floor. But the drawing influence of God's Word, its reasonableness, its beauty, the attractiveness of Christ revealed therein, must be the deciding influences, not our feelings.

> How can we possibly lead others to a full **assurance**, to simple, childlike faith in our heavenly Father, when we are measuring and judging our love to him by our feelings?[2]

♦ Further discussion on the above topic may be found in Chapter 10 under "Assurance and Feeling."

Paul learned the folly of resting his assurance in men, their conclusions, their beliefs, their instructions, who "professing themselves to be wise ... became fools."[3] He advised that "the foolishness of God is wiser than men.... God hath chosen the foolish things of the world to confound the wise ... that no flesh should glory in his [own] presence."[4]

> [On the road to Damascus, Saul the Pharisee] saw his folly in resting his faith upon the **assurances** of the priests and rulers, whose sacred office had given them great influence over his mind, and caused him to believe that the story of the resurrection was an artful fabrication of the disciples of Jesus.[5]

---

[1] *Signs of the Times*, 4-18-1895. ¶ 5. Italic added..

[2] *Ibid.*, 12-3-1894. ¶ 7.

[3] Romans 1:22.

[4] 1 Corinthians 1:25, 27, 29.

[5] *The Spirit of Prophecy*, III. 307.

Chapter 9

HOW DOES ONE GET ASSURANCE?

How is assurance generated in a world characterized by the lack of it? The citation of a few examples might help clarify the question: *How* does one go about obtaining an assurance such as David's when facing Goliath, or like that of the three Hebrew youth when confronted by the fiery furnace, or such as the prophet Elisha's when he was surrounded by the Syrian host at Dothan?

At one point in their duel to the death *both* Goliath and David *simultaneously* felt wholly assured of victory. Why? When only one could be the victor, how could both feel so fully confident of a favorable outcome? They certainly must have been basing their conclusions on different premises. Additional discussion on the David versus Goliath confrontation may be found in the introduction to this book.

From this, it seems clear that assurance can betray us, that it is not something on which to rely in times of crisis. It apparently also seemed rather obvious to both the Israelite and Philistine armies what the outcome would be, and it is also evident that both armies and their leaders felt quite assured of something totally wrong! It is a sad fact ·that in their minds, both armies were in agreement, when Israel should have been highly confident of a much different result than were the Philistines. It is important that we avoid Israel's mistake.

From all that we can tell, David was the only person at the battle front who was confident of an Israelite victory. But then, had Israel had faith in David's God, they wouldn't have been trembling before Goliath twice daily for forty days! His challenge would have been answered at his first appearance. There never would have been an opportunity or need for the manifestation of David's faith, or for that matter, for a king to replace Saul. One wonders where Jonathan and his armor-bearer were. Perhaps Jonathan needed this demonstration of David's faith to bring him up to full confidence in David's God.

Eleven centuries later, Saul, the intellectual Pharisee, felt fully assured that all Christians were subversive heretics and must be destroyed to preserve the true faith.[1] Later, known as Paul, he was so sure that Christ was the Messiah that he willingly submitted to the headsman's ax in testimony to his loyalty to the Christ whose influence he had been once so assured he must destroy.[2]

There have been many Davids, Goliaths, Sauls, and Pauls down through history. It is clear from these brief examples that assurance is a mixed bag. It was essential for David so that he could have calm nerves, a steady hand, and true aim as he directed that stone from his sling to its mark. For Goliath it proved his downfall as in proud over-confidence he raised his visor and exposed the one area vulnerable to David's well-slung and angel-guided stone.

Today, as we face the Goliaths stalking the land, and the Sauls in the vanguard of Christianity, we have a great

---

[1] Acts 7:58; 8:1; 9:1, 2.

[2] 2 Timothy 4:6-8.

advantage over David. He had some familiarity with Samuel, the prophet; but he had possibly never seen the scrolls written by Moses, who had died nearly four hundred years earlier. He was largely dependent on word-of-mouth transmission for his knowledge of God's instructions and promises. By contrast we have the 775,000 written words of the completed Bible, plus twenty-five times that volume of studied commentary by the "Comforter" on those sacred writings.

> The treasures of heaven will be opened to supply the wants of every hungering, thirsting soul. All of *this character* have the **assurance** of one day beholding the glory of that kingdom which as yet the imagination can only faintly grasp.[1]

Man cannot, out of thin air, generate an appetite for the "treasures of heaven." A bakery, to create an appetite for its wares and entice customers into the store, puts its fetching productions on display in the plate glass store window. God has put himself on display in Jesus Christ to create an insatiable appetite and unquenchable thirst for heavenly things. If I want to have "the assurance"—granted to "all of this character"—"of one day beholding the glory" of the heavenly kingdom I must fix the mind's eyes upon God's preview of this kingdom revealed in the transcendent birth, life, death, resurrection, and present ministry of His Son.

It is the privilege of all to have the assurance God provides, an advanced version of the assurance David had when facing Goliath, and which Paul had when facing the headsman's ax. We may all have that assurance possessed by the little Hebrew maid in the prophet of God when she was a slave in the household of Naaman the Syrian—"Would God my lord were with the prophet that is in Samaria! for he would

---

[1] *Signs of the Times*, 2-4-1897. ¶ 5. Emphases added.

recover him of his leprosy."[1] No hesitation. No doubts. She was fully assured that Elisha would heal this heathen Gentile enemy! But in spite of the availability of such assurance, almost all of us are supported by an assurance that is no better than that provided by the world, the kind possessed by Goliath and Saul the Pharisee. Most of us are characterized by an assurance—if we have any at all—of the human-generated, "I'm OK, you're OK" variety. Let us consider now how and where we may obtain something vastly superior to this broken reed upon which many of us are leaning.

6. ASSURANCE THROUGH HUMBLE REPENTANCE AND CONFESSION

> All who humble their hearts, confessing their sins, will find mercy and grace and **assurance**.[2]

Notice how incredibly simple and all-inclusive is the receiving of this blessing! Why then do so few possess it? Pride looms as the likely explanation.

> [David] confessed his sin, repented, and was reconverted. In the rapture of the **assurance** of forgiveness, he exclaimed: "Blessed is he whose transgression is forgiven, whose sin is covered."... The blessing comes because of pardon; pardon comes through faith that the sin, confessed and repented of, is borne by the great Sin Bearer.[3]

> Satan is ready to steal away the blessed **assurances** of God. He desires to take every glimmer of hope and every ray of light from the soul; but you must not permit him to do this. Do not give ear to the tempter, but say, "Jesus has died that I might live. He loves me, and wills not that I should perish. I have a compassionate heavenly Father; and although I

---

[1] 2 Kings 5:3.

[2] God's *Amazing Grace*, 136 (1904). Also in *The Bible Commentary*, VII, 931.

[3] *Our High Calling*, 83 (Ms 21, 1891).

have abused His love, though the blessings He has given me have been squandered, I will arise, and go to my Father, and say, 'I have sinned against heaven, and before Thee, and am no more worthy to be called Thy son: make me as one of Thy hired servants' [Luke 15:18, 19]."[1]

7. ASSURANCE THROUGH DEATH OF THE "OLD MAN" AND RE-BIRTH

Those who are converted, experience peace and **assurance** forever [Isaiah 32:17]. In place of being slaves, they are made free through Jesus Christ. Brought into the liberty of obedient children, they can say, "I delight in the law of God after the inward man" [Romans 7:22].[2]

God asserts here through Isaiah (32:17) that assurance is the "work" and "effect of righteousness," and that it is through being "converted" from the old man to the new that this experience is gained. It must be then that the re-birth of the Christian is a conversion to righteousness from unrighteousness, a transformation to right-doing from wrong-doing. The "old man" is a wrong-doer, the "new man" a right-doer. The experiential difference between law-abiding and law-breaking is "quietness and **assurance** forever"—the inward testimony of the Comforter—versus the state of the wicked who are described as being "like the troubled sea when it cannot rest.... There is no peace ... to the wicked."[3]

The converted soul can say, I needed help, and I found that help in Jesus. He has met every want, satisfied the hungering of my soul, and the Bible to me is the revelation of Jesus Christ. He can say to the infidel, "You ask me why I believe in Jesus? and I answer, Because he is to me a divine Saviour. The Bible to me is the voice of God. **I have the witness in myself** that the word of God is true,

---

[1] *Steps to Christ*, 53.

[2] *Signs of the Times*, 11-5-1894, ¶ 7.

[3] Isaiah 57:20, 21.

and that Jesus Christ is the divine Son of God. I am following no cunningly devised fable."[1]

David, Paul, and an army of like witnesses had this inward testimony; and so may we. The lack of this reassuring experience should say something to us about a need in us for a manifestation of grace, for a closer relationship to God, a need of rebirth, of putting off the old man and putting on the new, of becoming new creations so that "old things are passed away" and "all things are become new."[2]

8. ASSURANCE THROUGH THE WORD OF GOD

> They overcame ... by the blood of the lamb, and by the word of their testimony.[3]

John 6:53, 54, 63 make it clear that the "blood of the Lamb" by which we overcome is the life-giving Word. God's people overcome by God's Word and their own word of testimony concerning their experience in that Word. If we confess Jesus before men, He will confess us before His Father and the angels.[4] The fact that Jesus will confess His "friends" "before the angels" is a very reassuring thought. It was this that marshaled the angels ("chariots of fire") between Elisha and the Syrian army at Dothan, and enabled him to declare with calm assurance to his alarmed servant, "They that be with us are more than they that be with them."[5]

> We have an **assurance** that Jesus is our Saviour, and that we may draw freely from Him. We may partake freely of the rich provision that He has made for us in His Word. We may take Him at His word, believe on Him, and **know** that

---

[1] *Signs of the Times*, 9-3-1894, ¶ 4.

[2] 2 Corinthians 5:17.

[3] Revelation 12:11.

[4] Matthew 10:32; Luke 12:8.

[5] 2 Kings 6:16.

He will give us grace and power to do just as He bids us.
He has given us every **assurance**, and He will fulfill all that
He has promised.[1]

◆ Further discussion in this important area may be found in Chapters 6 and 8
under the topics "Assurance That God's Word Is True" and "Assurance Is
Found in God's Word Associated with Cheerful, Selfless Obedience."

9. ASSURANCE THROUGH FAITH

Whatsoever is born of God overcometh the world; and this
is the victory that overcometh the world, even our faith.[2]

Let us draw near [to God] with a true heart in full assurance
of faith.[3]

The expression, "Full assurance of faith" (or "Full
assurance of His faith"), occurs just this once in the
Bible, but is repeated scores of times in the further
testimonies of the Holy Spirit to the last days church of
Revelation 14:6-12. We have included a small sample of
these below (In these all emphasis is added). Certainly it is
evident that faith holds the key to the Christian's assurance.
"Without faith it is impossible to please him,"[4] and certainly
no one under the displeasure of God can possibly possess
true peace and assurance. However, there are counterfeits
that serve fairly well at holding fears and anxieties at arm's
length for a time. We have previously discussed examples of
these, such as found in the cases of Goliath, Peter, and Saul
the Pharisee.

Christ abiding in the heart will prompt right desires. Then
we may press to the mercy seat, and in the name of Jesus,

---

[1] *Sermons and Talks,* II. 293 (3-10-1908).

[2] 1 John 5:4.

[3] Hebrews 10:22.

[4] Hebrews 11:6.

our Advocate, in *the full **assurance** of faith,* claim all that the soul needs.[1]

[C]ome to God with *full **assurance** of faith,* knowing that he who hath promised is faithful, and will fulfill his word.... Fasten your soul on the blessed **assurance**, God has spoken this promise, God has invited me, not to mock me, not to disappoint me, for before I knocked, he was unlocking the door for me.[2]

We must receive His Word as spoken to us; and if we regard it thus, we shall come to the throne of grace with *full **assurance** of faith.*[3]

If the reader will make a search of the available EGW CD, he will find some seventy additional uses of this expression, "Full assurance of faith," or "Full assurance of his faith." Note that these two expressions are identical to the CD's search process, since "of" and "his" belong to a list of words (called stop words) that are non-existent to the search engine. In some respects, "full assurance of *his* faith" is less subject to misapplication, since there are many counterfeits out there that will finally produce nothing but fears and anxieties. Only the faith of Jesus will be accompanied by lasting assurance. It is "the faith of Jesus" that is possessed by God's last people in this present world.[4]

In Chapter 3 under the topic, "Assurance of Fulfilled Promises," we discussed two approaches to God: "If You *will*, you can"; and "If You *can*, will You?" These two approaches define the difference between faith and doubt, respectively. In the Bible's faith chapter (Hebrews 11), this same truth is presented in different words: "Without faith it is impossible to please him, for he that cometh to God must

---

[1] *Signs of the Times*, 12-28-1891, ¶ 3.
[2] *Ibid.*, 9-12-1892, ¶ 7.
[3] *Ibid.*, 5-19-1898, ¶ 1.
[4] Revelation 14:12.

believe that he is [that He *can*—is able], and that he is a rewarder of them that diligently seek him" (i.e. He will do what is asked by the one who believes He *can,* if it is His will—if it is for the good of the seeker, which means it is for the glory of His name). The seeker has the assurance that the best thing possible will happen to him, or for whomever his request is made. The following comments elaborate further upon this functional relationship between genuine faith and assurance:

> Personal faith in the efficacy of the blood of Christ in our own behalf, gives peace and **assurance** forever [Is. 32:17].[1]

> An unyielding trust, a firm reliance upon Christ, will bring peace and **assurance** to the soul.[2]

> We need not walk in **darkness**. We need not go on in **uncertainty**. We are willing to believe what our friends tell us, then why not believe the word of our best Friend?[3]

> Do you want a special feeling or emotion to prove that Christ is yours? Is this more reliable than pure faith in God's promises? Would it not be better to take the blessed promises of God and apply them to yourself, bearing your whole weight upon them? This is faith.... [W]e are to say, 'I believe thy promise, Lord, because thou hast said it. Thy word is pledged; we know that we are the children of God because we comply with the conditions, because he has pledged his word.' There is not a friend in the world of whom you would require one-half the **assurance** that our Heavenly Father has given you in his promises.[4]

> We must have faith, and walk by faith; not entertain the idea that we must have **assurance** in feeling before we

---

[1] *Review and Herald,* 7-14-1891, ¶ 4.

[2] *Ibid.,* 11-15-1887, ¶ 4 (Also in *Messages to Young People,* 112, and in *The Sanctified Life,* 90).

[3] *Signs of the Times,* 1-19-1891, ¶ 8.

[4] *Review and Herald,* 7-29-1890, ¶ 5.

acknowledge ourselves blessed of God. The **assurance** is in God's word. God has said, and it will be done.[1]

We must earnestly cry to God in faith, feeling or no feeling, and then live our prayers. Our **assurance** and evidence is God's word, and after we have asked we must believe without doubting.[2]

◆ For more on the relationship between faith and feeling see the topic, "Assurance and Feeling," in Chapter 10.

10. ASSURANCE THROUGH EARNEST, DIFFICULT EFFORT

There are those who imagine that they can secure heaven in an easy chair, that the path to heaven is an escalator or a helicopter ride, rather than the "narrow, shining steep" it is.[3] While there may be an ephemeral "assurance" in such concepts, it is built upon a foundation laid by the world, such as the assurance possessed by Goliath or by Saul, the brilliant, unconverted Pharisee, or by those described in Matthew 7:26 who build their character structures upon sand.

Let none imagine that without earnest effort on their part they can obtain the **assurance** of God's love. When the mind has been long permitted to dwell only on earthly things, it is a difficult matter to change the habits of thought.[4]

But take heart. "When the mind has been long permitted to dwell only on earthly things, it is a difficult matter to change the habits of thought," but *"habit will finally make it easy."*[5]

---

[1] *Ibid.,* 4-12-1887, ¶ 6.

[2] *Selected Messages,* II, 243 (Letter 7, 1892).

[3] "Everyone is permitted to choose for himself the narrow, shining steep that leads to heaven, or that broader and easier way which ends in death." —*Signs of the Times,* 1-26-1882, ¶ 3. Also in *Our High Calling,* 11.

[4] *Review and Herald,* 11-15-1887, ¶ 8. Also in *Messages to Young People,* 113, and in *The Sanctified Life,* 91f.

[5] *Ibid.,* 11-15-1887, ¶ 11. Italic added.

It takes power, power that we should be aware of, to climb the narrow, steep heavenward path. Habit does not reduce the effort required, but it can cause it to become more natural to put forth those powers of human effort bestowed upon us by the grace of God. To refuse to use them is to abuse them. Do not allow the carnal desire for ease to lead you to sink down into do-nothingness, but get up out of Satan's comfortable easy chair[1] and join with Christ in using the gifts of God's grace to "work out your ... salvation, with fear and trembling."[2]

> When you indulge the feelings of the natural heart, letting the carnal nature have the supremacy, then ... what **assurance** have you that you are kept by the power of God unto salvation?[3]

11. ASSURANCE THROUGH SURRENDER

> Trust in the Lord with all thine heart; and lean not unto thine own understanding. In all thy ways acknowledge him, and he shall direct thy paths.[4]

There is no power in humanity and no assurance in human leadership. If I submit to human control or insist on following my own way, I will find nothing but weakness. Such a powerless state can provide no assurance. There is a better way.

> [W]hen we submit to God's way, the Lord Jesus guides our minds and fills our lips with **assurance**.[5]

> Only in humble reliance upon God, and obedience to all His commandments, can we be **secure**.[1]

---

[1] "Do not sit down in Satan's easy-chair of do-little, but arise, and aim at the elevated standard which it is your privilege to attain." —*Testimonies for the Church*, I, 241.

[2] Philippians 2:12, 13.

[3] *Review and Herald*, 3-8-1892 ¶ 8 (Talk, 7-23-1891).

[4] Proverbs 3:5, 6.

[5] *Testimonies for the Church*, VII, 71.

Entire surrender of your ways, which seem so very wise, and taking Christ's ways, is the secret of perfect **rest** in His love.[2]

And if surrender, there must be a ruler to whom we surrender, and a ruler-subject relationship. This brings us to the next topic.

12. ASSURANCE THROUGH A REDEEMER-RULER-SUBJECT RELATIONSHIP

Not everyone that saith unto me, Lord, Lord, shall enter into the kingdom of heaven, but he that doeth the will of my Father.... Afterward came also the [foolish] virgins, saying, Lord, Lord, open to us. But he answered and said ... I know you not.... And why call ye me, Lord, Lord, and do not the things which I say?[3]

God's Chosen People of Christ's day wanted a ruler Messiah, a Messiah who would rule sternly over their enemies, the Gentiles, and who would retain the haughty Jewish rulers in their positions of power and keep the poor of the land in their positions of ignorance, insecurity and subservience. The Jewish leaders did not want a Redeemer, a Restorer who would break down the caste barriers between rich and poor, between the powerful and the weak, even of Jewry. They would brook no interference with their authority over the chattels under their control. They simply wanted their dictatorship to be extended to the Gentiles and were unattracted by the kingdom which Jesus came to establish—a rulership of love and humility.

In our day there are many who are quite happy to have a Redeemer to spare them the consequences of sinning, but

---

[1] *The Great Controversy* (1911 edition), 530.

[2] *Manuscript Releases*, XXI. 230 (Letter 130, 1898, to Elder and Sister S. N. Haskell; may also be found in part in *My Life Today*, 176).

[3] Matthew 7:21; 25:11, 12; Luke 6:46.

who do not wish Him to rule over them. In our human nature it is natural to rebel against anyone's assuming the right to tell us what to do, to make rules by which we are expected to behave, rules for which at times we may not even be able to see the reasons. But this is how sin entered; and the author would like to show that if this situation is to be corrected, if we are to have Jesus as our Redeemer, we must *by choice* also have Him as our Ruler. Until we are fully settled on this point we cannot pass through the gates of a city in which Jesus, our Redeemer, is King. Man's unsettled state on this issue is the very reason that causes him to lack assurance of eternal security.

> Let this point be fully settled in every mind: *If we accept Christ as a Redeemer, we must accept Him as a Ruler.* We cannot have the **assurance** and perfect confiding trust in Christ as our Saviour until we acknowledge Him as our King and are obedient to His commandments.[1]

This much is clear—unless there is a way to be redeemed apart from Christ, no such thing exists as a person who is saved and who is making his own rules of behavior! Saying the same thing in another way—no one can with assurance address Jesus as Lord who has assumed lordship of himself! He can choose to take over the rule-making process, but he cannot do so and retain his soteriological ("salvational") standing before God. He cannot replace God as his ruler and retain the assurance that Jesus is his Saviour. *This* is an issue that must be *"fully settled in every mind."* The following testimony of the Spirit concisely expresses in a nutshell this ruler–acceptance (of Christ) concept, and its relationship to assurance:

---

[1] *Faith and Works*, 16 (Ms 36, 1890). Emphases added.

ASSURANCE—HOW DOES ONE GET IT?

When Christ *reigns* in the soul, there is purity, freedom from sin.... The *acceptance* of the Saviour brings a glow of perfect peace, perfect love, perfect **assurance**.[1]

One of the great advantages we have when we acquire Jesus as Redeemer is that we then have a Leader, our King, who knows where all the land-mines are in that precarious pathway to heaven. Many years ago I went spelunking (cave exploring) with a friend in Tennessee. He knew the cave we were exploring very well, and for that I was very thankful because after we had been in there for about an hour while he led us through this and that passageway in total darkness, except for our flashlights, sometimes barely squeezing through, and at times coming upon precipitous vertical drops that must be avoided, I began to silently criticize myself for not bringing along a couple of sets of extra flashlight batteries. But always there was the reassuring thought that my companion knew the way around all the hazards and how to get out! Then suddenly we saw daylight, and all my unexpressed apprehensions were gone. This world is a dark, confusing, misleading maze. But we have our reassuring Redeemer-Ruler (Leader) who has gone down every path and sailed every sea lane. We need a pilot, He knows the way through!

Though multitudes are pressing on in the wrong way, though the outlook be ever so discouraging, yet we may have full **assurance** in our Leader; for 'I am God,' he declares, 'and there is none else' [Isaiah 45:22; 46:9, &c].[2]

13. ASSURANCE THROUGH ABIDING IN CHRIST

This topic has been presented in the Introduction and further discussed in Chapter Two under the heading, "Assurance of an Intimately Present, Abiding Christ." There we were

[1] *Christ's Object Lessons,* 420. Emphases added.
[2] *Review and Herald,* 6-9-1910, ¶ 9.

172

discussing a list of thirty-six things which are an incomplete partial answer to the question, "Of what are we assured?" Here we are seeking an answer to the question, "How do we obtain assurance?" We offer here some evidence of the importance of maintaining this close relationship described as abiding in Christ as a means of obtaining assurance.

> See that your life is hid with Christ in God [Colossians 3:3], and you will be filled with the most precious **assurance** that you are a child of Heaven.[1]

> Those who have a vital union with Christ will rejoice in the **assurance** of his love.[2]

> Christ abiding in the heart will prompt right desires. Then we may press to the mercy seat, and in the name of Jesus, our Advocate, in the full **assurance** of faith, claim all that the soul needs....

> "If ye keep my commandments, ye shall abide in my love; even as I have kept my Father's commandments, and abide in his love." Here again the Lord Jesus presents his relationship to the Father as the exact counterpart of our relationship to himself. Let these lessons, so full of instruction, be carefully considered. Nowhere else can be found such large and comforting **assurances**.[3]

14. ASSURANCE THROUGH PARTAKING OF THE DIVINE NATURE

> Ever learning of the divine Teacher, daily partaking of his nature, we cooperate with God in overcoming Satan's temptations. God works, and man works, that man may be one with Christ as Christ is one with God. Then we sit together with Christ in heavenly places [Ephesians 2:6]. The mind rests with peace and **assurance** in Jesus.[4]

---

[1] *Ibid.*, 8-14-1888. ¶ 9.
[2] *Ibid.*, 2-15-1887. ¶ 6.
[3] *Signs of the Times*, 12-28-1891. ¶ 11.
[4] *Review and Herald*, 4-24-1900. ¶ 7.

♦ See the subtopic "Assurance of Divine Nature" in Chapter 7 for further discussion on this incredible privilege offered to all who will receive it.

15. ASSURANCE THROUGH PRAISE AND REJOICING IN GOD

If we would give more expression to our faith, rejoice more in the blessings that we know we have—the great mercy, forbearance, and love of God—we would daily have greater strength. Have not the precious words spoken by Christ, the Prince of God, an **assurance** and power that should have great influence upon us?[1]

16. ASSURANCE THROUGH CULTIVATING RIGHT PURPOSES

The words in favor of truth spoken with the **assurance** that comes from the possession of a right purpose, and in cheerful hope, from a pure heart, will make the angels rejoice.[2]

17. ASSURANCE THROUGH RECEIVING CHRIST'S RIGHTEOUSNESS

This title is not just a duplication, in different words, of the topic above, "Assurance Through Partaking of the Divine Nature"; although the first, above, is essential for the second, and the second, here, is an inevitable consequence of the first. They are an inseparable pair.

The fruit of righteousness is quietness and **assurance** forever [Isaiah 32:17].[3]

---

[1] *Selected Messages,* II, 243 (Letter 7, 1892).

[2] *Sons and Daughters of God,* 276 (1908).

[3] *Signs of the Times,* 10-4-1899, ¶ 6.

Desire the fulness of the grace of Christ. Let your heart be filled with an intense longing for His righteousness, the work of which God's word declares is peace, and its effect quietness and **assurance** forever [Isaiah 32:17].[1]

We are to put into practice the precepts of the law, and thus have righteousness before us; the rearward will be God's glory. The light of the righteousness of Christ will be our front guard, and the glory of the Lord will be our rearward [Isaiah 58:8]. Let us thank the Lord for this **assurance**.[2]

18. HOW NOT TO OBTAIN ASSURANCE

The Scriptures have left us with many examples of unjustified assurance—"assurance" obtained by inappropriate reasoning. We have already discussed some of these such as Goliath and Saul of Tarsus. Some of the following have already been quoted in the last section of Chapter 8. Because of its appropriateness, it is used again here.

There are efforts made in our own strength, but there is not a dying to self, the soul is not surrendered to God. Many are making a mistake here. They are hoping to overcome through their own efforts, and by *their* goodness gain the **assurance** of the love of God. They do not exercise faith; they do not believe that Jesus accepts their repentance and contrition, and so they toil on day after day without finding rest or peace.[3]

There are those who lack assurance that they have a right standing before God. This results from a disposition to stand on their own merits, rather than casting their helpless souls on the merits, love, and mercy of Christ.

I have listened to testimonies like this: "I have not the light that I desire; I have not the **assurance** of the favor of God."... Are you expecting that your merit will recommend

---

[1] *The Acts of the Apostles*, 566.

[2] *Selected Messages*, I, 99 (Sermon, 1-23-04: also in *Notebook Leaflets*, "The Church," Number 7).

[3] *Review and Herald*, 5-20-1884 ¶ 5 (Morning talk to ministers, 1883 General Conference).

you to the favor of God, and that you must be free from sin before you trust his power to save?[1]

---

[1] *Ibid.*, 4-22-1884, ¶ 5.

PART THREE

NON-CAUSE-EFFECT
ASSURANCE
RELATIONSHIPS

Chapter 10

ODDS AND ENDS OF ASSURANCE

We have discussed some of those things of which the Christian may be assured, where this assurance is found, and how it may be obtained. There are other assurance relationships which contain elements that do not easily fit into any of these categories. As in the first three classes, they often overlap to some extent with one or more of the others.

1. ASSURANCE AND THE WORD OF GOD

> Be **assured** that the Word of God will not fail.[1]

One will certainly be lacking in assurance if he is dwelling in spiritual darkness. It is natural to be "afraid of the dark," and spiritual darkness can be more terrifying than physical darkness because the latter deals with finite time but the former with eternity. It is possible while probation lasts to turn on the spiritual lights where they are off and come out into the light, a very reassuring experience.

> Those who do accept the evidences of God's word will have an experience that will be as a barrier against infidelity, for they will be *translated* out of darkness into the precious

---
[1] *Ibid.,* 5-21-1908, ¶ 5.

light of faith, hope, and **assurance**. The converted soul can say, I needed help, and I found that help in Jesus.... The Bible to me is the voice of God. **I have the witness in myself** that the word of God is true, and that Jesus Christ is the divine Son of God.[1]

It is [God's] will that you should go to the source of all light, and receive the enlightenment of His Spirit (for this will be given to every humble seeker for truth), and then you will know that the Spirit and the Word agree, and know that you know what is truth. What **assurance** this knowledge gives![2]

2. ASSURANCE AND MATURITY

Assurance in those thirty-six categories of Part 1, do not happen in an instant. There is a long period of growth before one reaches the place where he can face the headsman's ax and say with Paul, without apprehension, "I am now ready to be offered, and the time of my departure is at hand. I have fought a good fight, I have finished my course, I have kept the faith."[3] To Paul this was just another "light affliction which ... worketh for us a far more exceeding and eternal weight of glory."[4] He had assurance!

Were we to ground our hope upon joyful emotions, there are many of God's true people who would be without **assurance**. There are in the fold ... not only the sheep ... but the lambs.... If all had **strong assurance**, in what would the babe differ from those of more advanced experience? The word of God is rich in pearls of promises; but there are weak and trembling souls, who dare not venture to think that they are bringing forth fruit meet for repentance, and who fail to appropriate the promise; yet they are precious in the sight of the Lord....

---

[1] *Signs of the Times*, 9-3-1894, ¶ 4.

[2] *Counsels on Sabbath School Work*, 33.

[3] 2 Timothy 4:6, 7.

[4] 2 Corinthians 4:17.

> It would be the ruin of many a soul always to have **unclouded assurance** in joyful feelings that they are accepted of God. Without feeling we must learn to lean upon his word. We must learn to grasp the promise, because we can never perish if we come to the feet of infinite Love. The **absolute assurance** will be ours when we hear from the lips of the Master the welcome words, 'Well done, thou good and faithful servant;... enter thou into the joy of thy Lord' [Matthew 25:21, 23].[1]

But does not this coin have another side?

> We must have that faith in God that takes him at his word. We can have no victory without **cloudless confidence**; for 'without faith it is impossible to please' God [Hebrews 11:6].[2]

This sounds like we can have no victory until we have reached full maturity as Christians; but how can we mature without gaining victories? How can we reconcile this apparent conflict above between (1) "unclouded assurance" (which might be "the ruin of many"), on the one hand; and (2) "cloudless confidence" (without which "we can have no victory"), on the other; and (3) the assurance that "since it was the Spirit of God that inspired the Bible, it is impossible that the teaching of the Spirit should ever be contrary to that [teaching of the same Spirit] of the Word"?[3] It appears, at first inspection, that at least one of these three concepts cannot be the teaching of the Spirit. However, this illusion of conflict disappears, in the opinion of the author of this book, by noting that (1) refers to "unclouded assurance in *joyful feelings*," which is based in feeling—an inappropriate expectation; whereas (2) refers to "cloudless *confidence*," grounded, not in feeling, but in

---

[1] *Signs of the Times*, 4-18-1895. ¶ 2.

[2] *Review and Herald*, 1-10-1888. ¶ 10.

[3] *The Great Controversy* (1911 edition). vii.

"faith," a perfectly proper expectation. The next topic elaborates further on "Assurance and Feeling."

It is possible for us to *know* that we are maturing toward that "strong assurance" described above, that distinguishes "babes ... from those of more advanced experience."

> If you delight to dwell upon the plan of salvation, upon the glorious manifestations of the divine character, if your heart, in contemplation of the love of God, glows with thankfulness and joy, you may **be sure** that you have been illuminated by the beams of the Holy Spirit, and heavenly agencies are bringing your character up to maturity of Christian life.[1]

♦ For further, quite relevant, discussion on this subject see the topic, "Assurance of Growth," in Chapter 5.

3. ASSURANCE AND FEELING

The very word, "assurance," suggests a sense of well-being, a feeling as it were, that all is well. It is incompatible with another word—fear (of danger). Although the Christian's experience is not defined by his feelings, it is inevitable that as his closeness to God develops he will *feel* less and less vulnerable to the world's perils. He will be less and less concerned about what men or devils can do to him. A ring of courage, of fearlessness, will develop in his speaking. But the qualities of bravado and arrogance, will be absent. It is as if in our experience there is a rheostat under God's control by which God keeps increasing the electrifying experience referred to as "assurance." The believer will have more and more of Elisha's they-that-be-with-us-are-more-than-they-that-be-with-them experience, until he can with imperturbable inward calm say with Paul, "I am ready," "I am ready to be offered."

---

[1] *Signs of the Times*, 3-27-1893, ¶ 6.

A *feeling* of **assurance** is not to be despised; we should praise God for it; but when your feelings are depressed, do not think that God has changed. Praise Him just as much, because you *trust* in His word, and not in feelings [the Word has not changed!].[1]

The following illustrates this rheostat quality of assurance in which as one grows to Christian maturity, the power of assurance becomes stronger and stronger until finally, like the apostle Paul who while faced with imminent shipwreck, calmly sat down to eat,[2] so the Christian also enjoys imperturbable calmness of spirit under all the trying circumstances of life.

It is the privilege of God's people to go forth to their work in the strength of Jesus. We should go forth, not depending upon our talents, but wrestling with God for sanctification through the truth. We should *feel* a constant **assurance** that Jesus is present to help us.[3]

God keeps turning up the rheostat for the sense of security, the awareness that we are no longer fledglings but that we are full-fledged members of the family of God. We are no longer orphans. The result is more and more electrified Christians.

The reason that so large a number of those who profess to be children of God always feel in **uncertainty**, is because they feel that they are orphans. They do not cultivate the precious **assurance** that Jesus is the sin-bearer; that although they have transgressed the law, and are sinners in his sight, yet the object of the incarnation of Christ was to bring to the repenting, believing sinner everlasting peace and **assurance**.[4]

---

[1] *Our High Calling,* 124 (Letter 42, 1890). Emphases added.
[2] Acts 27:35.
[3] *Signs of the Times,* 3-31-1890, ¶ 4. Italic added.
[4] *Ibid.,* 11-12-1896, ¶ 9.

If we do not have ecstatic feelings, we begin to doubt whether we are Christians or not, when we should not look at our feelings, but at God's word; for there is our **assurance**.[1]

We are to find the **assurance** of our acceptance with God in his written promise, not in a happy flight of feeling[2]

The preceding and following make it clear that there is a notable distinction between joy, described as "a happy flight of feeling," and joy which is that more solid feeling of assurance "that the promises of God are still yea and amen in Christ Jesus." The promises "do not rest upon ["a happy flight of"] feeling." But the Christian's experience that results from resting on the promises should be characterized by the positive quality, peace, which cannot be divorced from the feelings. This positive, active quality leads one to rebuke the storms in his own life and makes him an agent in rebuking the storms in the lives of others.[3]

Suppose that at times we are destitute of the joy we should like to experience, can we not *feel* **assured** that the promises of God are still yea and amen in Christ Jesus [2 Corinthians 1:20]? The promises of God do not rest upon feeling. They have a foundation as distinct from feeling as light is from darkness.[4]

◆ More on the relationship between feeling and faith may be found under "Assurance Through Faith" in Chapter 9.

---

[1] *Review and Herald,* 4-12-1887, ¶ 7.

[2] *Signs of the Times,* 4-18-1895, ¶ 1.

[3] "Thou wilt keep him in *perfect peace* whose mind is stayed on thee" (Isaiah 26:3). "My peace I give unto you" (John 14:27). Cf. Mark 4:37-39. See also *Gospel Workers,* 1892 edition, 415: "God will accept every one that comes to him trusting wholly in the merits of a crucified Saviour.... There may be no *ecstasy* of feeling, *but there is an abiding, peaceful trust.*" Note that while there may be no *ecstasy* of feeling, there is an abiding *peaceful* feeling.

[4] *Signs of the Times,* 11-11-1889, ¶ 5 (Minneapolis, 10-19-1888). Italic added.

4. ASSURANCE AND HAPPINESS

The greatest assurance of happiness we can have is the assurance of God's love, a perpetual, ever-intensifying love-fest with God through His only begotten Son, the *man* Christ Jesus. This delightful experience is discussed more in Chapter 2 under the topic, "Assurance of Love," and in Chapter 7 under "Assurance of Happiness." A few additional thoughts on the relationship between assurance and happiness are added here.

God "delights in our happiness." In fact it was in happiness that He "created man for happiness," and He felt "very good" about what He had done. He "has bountifully provided for" man's happiness, and "desires that we shall constantly be growing" in it.[1] Happiness is one of those qualities of life God has designed shall increase without bound—through all eternity, an inviting concept.

Above the topic, "Assurance and Feeling," along with its relationship to joy was touched upon. There certainly is feeling in happiness—both the giddy, superficial worldly cover-up that depends on stimulation of the five senses by sitcoms, low blows called jokes, gourmet foods, sexual promiscuity called love, human praise, money, &c; and then that deeply satisfying kind that "doeth good like a medicine" and makes a "cheerful [but not silly] countenance."[2] God is constantly seeking the happiness of all His creatures; and it should come as no surprise that happiness is a component of just about everything God does, and this will certainly be a fact of life once the universe gets beyond the unwelcome intruder, Satan, and his uninvited co-conspirators.

---

[1] *Counsels to Parents, Teachers, and Students*, 188; *Christ's Object Lessons*, 290; *Counsels on Diet and Foods*, 20; *The Ministry of Healing*, 398.

[2] Proverbs 17:22; 15:13.

The Christian is not morose, sullen, and desponding; he is the happiest man in the world. He feels **secure**; for he trusts in Jesus, and enjoys his presence.[1]

The commandment-keeping people of God are to walk in the sunlight of Christ's righteousness, their countenances expressing cheerfulness and thanksgiving, joyful in the **assurance**, "Blessed are they that do his commandments, that they may have right to the tree of life, and may enter in through the gates into the city" [Revelation 22:14].[2]

To bring us once again to the ever delightful subject of love, we repeat:

[God] would have [His children] ... find greatest joy in the **assurance** of his great love wherewith he has loved us.[3]

5. ASSURANCE AND LOVE

Since "God is love," and the experience of loving and being loved is a such a pleasure, God has described it as a glowing, transcending experience and has made "perfect love" and "perfect assurance" equal elements in the same sentence, which we now quote:

The acceptance of the Saviour brings a glow of perfect peace, perfect love, perfect **assurance**.[4]

As might be expected, Satan has a counterfeit which takes on many colors, shapes, and forms. One of these is "self-love" which leads to unjustified self-assurance.

When Peter said he would follow his Lord to prison and to death, he meant it, every word of it;[5] but he did not know himself. Hidden in his heart were elements of evil that

---

[1] *Review and Herald,* 6-10-1884, ¶ 11 (Morning talk, 1883 General Conference).

[2] *Ibid.,* 5-3-1898, ¶ 14.

[3] *Signs of the Times,* 4-4-1895, ¶ 5.

[4] *Christ's Object Lessons,* 420.

[5] Clearly, Peter was *self-assured* of his love for, and loyalty to, Jesus.

circumstances would fan into life. Unless he was made conscious of his danger, these would prove his eternal ruin. The Saviour saw in him a self-love and **assurance** that would overbear even his love for Christ.... Peter needed to distrust himself, and to have a deeper faith in Christ.[1]

It is clear from the above declaration that Peter had a marked love of self, a level of self-assurance somewhat similar to that possessed by Goliath, the Philistine giant. Contrast this with the total absence of self-assurance in the man, Christ Jesus. His assurance was totally in a power outside of self. It was in His Father. In the storm-on-Galilee experience, the disciples could have stilled the sea had they had faith. Jesus said to them:

> Whosoever shall say unto this mountain, Be thou removed, and be thou cast into the sea; and shall not doubt in his heart, but shall believe that those things which he saith shall come to pass; he shall have whatsoever he saith.[2]

The issue was not who was the most powerful, Jesus or the disciples, for both were of themselves powerless to do anything—"I can [of myself] do nothing"; "Ye can [of yourselves] do nothing."[3] *"He rested not in the possession of almighty power.... That power He had laid down."*[4] There was a precise equivalence between what Jesus (the man) and the disciples could do of themselves, and what Jesus (the man) and the disciples could do through a Power outside of themselves—God. Joshua provides a remarkable example of the latter—"Sun, stand thou still upon Gibeon; and thou, Moon, in the valley of Ajalon.... So the sun stood still ... a

---

[1] *The Desire of Ages*, 673.

[2] Mark 11:23.

[3] John 5:30; 15:5.

[4] *The Desire of Ages*, 336.

whole day.”[1] This was certainly at least the equivalent of telling the air (wind) to stand still on the Sea of Galilee!

We notice that when Jesus, in the sinking boat, was awakened He did not pick up the oars! By picking up a pair of oars He could have made an 8% difference in their struggle with the storm. By the course He pursued, He made an infinite difference. Jesus' question to them—“Where is your faith?”[2]—implies that they could have been the same instruments of peace that He was; but, no, their “faith” was in their experience and prowess with the oars—that is, in themselves. This was all too Goliath-like! Jesus' faith was not at all in Himself, but in His Father, and *our* Father.

> Those who truly love God have **internal evidence** [assurance!] that they are beloved of God, that they have communion with Christ, that their hearts are warmed with fervent love toward him.[3]

> His love is like a vast ocean, without bottom or shore. In all true disciples this love, like sacred fire, burns on the altar of the heart.[4]

6. ASSURANCE AND CONFIDENCE (FAITH)

To the Christian everything is of faith, because “whatsoever is not of faith is sin.”[5] Consequently this topic overlaps just about all the others. However, although some of what is presented here has already appeared in other areas of this book, it is repeated because this is where some may rightly expect to find it.

---

[1] Joshua 10:12.

[2] Luke 8:25.

[3] *Review and Herald,* 5-12-1896, ¶ 7.

[4] *Lift Him Up,* 248.

[5] Romans 14:23.

Our faith and assurance in God will be severely tested. We must get to know God well and Jesus as our personal Saviour if we are to pass that final examination. There is still time to make the necessary preparation.

> There were many who at first received Noah's message, but the fear of men was greater than the fear of God, and they turned away from the truth of God to believe a lie.... It is the testing time that will measure professed faith and **assurance** in God.[1]

> His every word and look invite our **confidence**.[2]

It is not too late—yet—to prepare, but the fact that time is indeed running out is urged upon us.

> [I]t is not too late to examine our own hearts, and prove ourselves, whether we are in the faith or not [2 Corinthians 13:5]; it is not too late to **assure** ourselves that Christ is abiding in our heart [*sic*] by faith.[3]

Faith will assure us that while God is to be "feared," He is at the same time, most approachable.

> [C]ome to God with *full* **assurance** of faith, knowing that he who hath promised is faithful, and will fulfill his word.[4]

> [The Lord] bids His believing saints to advance unitedly, going from strength to greater strength, from faith to increased **assurance** and confidence in the truth and righteousness of His cause.[5]

Faith can provide no genuine assurance unless there is evidence in the life that the creative power of God has been exercised upon mind and heart in bringing into existence a new creature in His own likeness.

---

[1] *Signs of the Times*, 4-18-1895, ¶ 8.

[2] *Review and Herald*, 10-30-1900, ¶ 12.

[3] *Ibid.*, 8-27-1889, ¶ 1 (Chicago, 4-9-1889).

[4] *Signs of the Times*, 9-12-1892, ¶ 7.

[5] *Review and Herald*, 6-12-1913, ¶ 19 (Also in *Selected Messages*, II, 407).

How can we come to God with full **assurance** of faith if we bear no fruit that testifies to a change wrought in us by the grace of God?... None of us need walk in **uncertainty**.[1]

◆ For further discussion of the relationship between assurance and faith see in this chapter under "Assurance and Feeling" and in Chapter 9 under "Assurance Through Faith."

7. ASSURANCE AND POWER

The author has some 180 computer files that are compilations of inspired statements on different topics. The largest of these by a considerable margin is the compilation on "Power" including strength, force, energy, and sufficiency. That compilation consists of about 140 pages of more than 700 statements. This is quite interesting when one considers that in this list of compilations are other very frequently addressed topics such as "Faith (Belief, Confidence, Trust)," "Grace," "The Holy Spirit," "Love," "Salvation," "Sanctification," "Union" [with God and other believers], "Witnessing." What this says is that power is a very fundamental and essential component of the redemption process. God would not otherwise devote such a large proportion of the redemption effort to the discussion of it. And we need to spend a large part of our time listening to what God spends a large part of the time He has devoted to humanity saying. David had such assurance in his face-off with Goliath because he had spent so much time listening to the powerful voice of God while tending "those few sheep in the wilderness."[2] The following suggests that Christ's righteousness raises our level of assurance because it is a *garment* of power:

---

[1] *EGW 1888 Materials,* 132 (Sunday, 10-21-1888).

[2] I Samuel 17:28.

One sentence of scripture is of more value than ten thousand of man's ideas or arguments.... But when we submit to God's way, the Lord Jesus guides our minds and fills our hearts with **assurance**. We may be strong in the Lord and in the power of His might. Receiving Christ, we are *clothed* with power.[1]

The **assurance** that we are under the protection of Omnipotence [the all-powerful God] imparts courage and **confidence**, inspires a hope that is 'as an anchor of the soul, both sure and steadfast, and which entereth into that within the vail' [Hebrews 6:19]. This **assurance** is a source of strength unknown to the worldling or to the half-hearted professor.[2]

We are nearing the end of this book, and we have seen an incredible list of assurances with which God has hedged us in. There are yet many other ways, "a thousand ways,"[3] by which God wishes to remove our anxieties and to fill us with hope, confidence, and courage. The possession of "all power"[4] enables Jesus to provide us with "*every* assurance."

We may take Him at His word, believe on Him, and know that He will give us grace and power to do just as He bids us. He has given us every **assurance**, and He will fulfill all that He has promised.[5]

All this assurance has been provided, and yet so many go through life in uncertainty, fearing disaster may await them at the next curve. There is a correctable reason for this:

When you indulge the feelings of the natural heart, letting the carnal nature have the supremacy, then I ask, What **assurance** have you that you are kept by the power of God unto salvation?[6]

---

[1] *Testimonies for the Church*, VII, 71. Emphases added.

[2] *Signs of the Times*, 1-28-1886, ¶ 10.

[3] *The Desire of Ages*, 330.

[4] Matthew 28:18.

[5] *Sermons and Talks*, II, 293.

[6] *Review and Herald*, 3-8-1892, ¶ 7 (Talk, 7-23-91).

8. ASSURANCE AND PRAYER

One may think of effective prayer as having three components—trust, fervor, and assurance. When these are present they testify to the world and the universe of two facts—(1) one's belief in God, and (2) that one has made Christ his personal Saviour.

> The prayer of faith is not listless, dry, and uninteresting. It wells up from perfect trust and **assurance**, and by its fervor makes manifest to the world, to angels, and to men, that you do believe in God, and have made Christ your personal Saviour.[1]

Before we leave this subject of assurance and prayer we slightly crack the door in defining more clearly what it means to have trust, fervor, and assurance in prayer, prayer that not only moves the hearts of men but the arm of God, prayer that demonstrates what it means to come to God with "full **assurance** of faith."[2]

> "Verily, verily, I say unto you, He that believeth on Me, the works that I do shall he do also; and greater works than these shall he do [through the grace and power of Christ]; because I go unto My Father. And whatsoever ye shall ask in My name, that will I do, that the Father may be glorified in the Son. If ye shall ask anything in My name, I will do it" [John 14:12-14].... This promise was spoken by lips that never deceived, and we must take the pledged Word of God and believe it, and act upon it. We must receive His Word as *spoken*[3] to us; and *if we regard it thus,* we shall come to the throne of grace with full **assurance** of faith.[4]

---

[1] *Signs of the Times,* 6-18-1896, ¶ 7.

[2] Hebrews 10:22.

[3] "The Scriptures are to be received as God's word to us, *not written merely, but spoken....* In them He is speaking to us *individually,* speaking as directly as if we could listen to His voice." —*The Ministry of Healing,* 122. Italic added.

[4] *Signs of the Times,* 5-19-1898, ¶ 1. Bracketed phrase in the original. Emphases added.

Trust, fervor, and assurance, certainly carry the implication that prayer is not to be feelingless. "It wells up" to overflowing in a way that cannot be restrained. "Assurance" and "fervor" carry that meaning in a way that "trust" does not. We are to pray with the *threesome,* "trust, fervor and assurance"—with both faith and feeling. In the story of Luke 11 of the need for bread at midnight, and in the parable of the widow and the unjust judge of Luke 18, the requests are presented with great urgency, feeling, and persistence. The suppliants will not be denied. It is as Matthew records Jesus: "The kingdom of heaven suffereth violence, and the violent take it by force."[1] "The effectual, *fervent* prayer of a righteous man availeth much."[2]

"We need to know how to pray. It is not tame, spiritless prayers that take hold of the divine attributes."[3] "It is generally the case that the less of heaven's vitality there is in a prayer, the more lengthy it is.... Let the prayers made in public be short and *full of earnestness....* Let there be a revival of the Holy Spirit, that your prayers may be filled with the power of heaven."[4] Every prayer should have the ring of faith and assurance. Other prayers "might better not be uttered."[5]

9. ASSURANCE AND THE HOLY SPIRIT

The subject of the relationship between assurance and the Holy Spirit is very broad and can be treated in only a very limited way in this book which we are committed to keeping small. Some treatment on that subject may be found in Chapter 4 under the topic, "Assurance of Receiving the Holy

---

[1] Matthew 11:12.

[2] James 5:16. Italic added.

[3] *In Heavenly Places,* 75.

[4] *Review and Herald,* 1-14-1902. ¶ 11. Italic added.

[5] *Counsels to Parents, Teachers, and Students,* 243.

Spirit." Here we have briefly added some additional counsel that could not be included there.

> [T]he divine **assurance** which [Christ's disciples] manifested [after Pentecost] was an evidence to men that they had received the gift of the Holy Ghost. Men's hearts were melted and subdued. The promise, "Greater works than these shall he do" [John 14:12], was fulfilled.[1]

> The Comforter is given that he may take of the things of Christ and show them unto us, that he may present in their rich **assurance** the words that fell from his lips, and convey them with living power to the soul who is obedient, who is emptied of self.[2]

10. ASSURANCE AND FEAR

> When Jesus was awakened to meet the storm [Matthew 8:25], He was in perfect peace. There was no trace of fear in word or look, for no fear was in His heart. But *He rested not in the possession of almighty power....* He trusted in the Father's might.[3]

This is a wonderful assurance for us—that "He rested not in" His own divine power (because we have none!), but "in the Father's might," in which *we may also rest.* In His reaction to this life-threatening storm, He had no advantage over us![4] His reaction to the storm was rather an *example* for us. "Christ also suffered for us, leaving us an example that [we] should follow his steps."[5]

---

[1] *Review and Herald,* 6-18-1895, ¶ 7.

[2] *Signs of the Times,* 12-25-1893, ¶ 5.

[3] *The Desire of Ages,* 336. Italic added.

[4] "[D]ivine power was not given to Him in a different way to what it will be given to us." —*The Bible Commentary,* VII, 925 (Ms 21, 1895). "Jesus resisted the temptations of Satan in the same manner in which every tempted soul may resist the evil.... Every man may overcome as Christ overcame.... If Christ had a special power which it is not the privilege of a[nother] man to have, Satan would have made capital of this matter. —*Signs of the Times,* 4-10-1893, ¶ 2, 3.

[5] 1 Peter 2:21.

Those who are true to God need not fear the power of men nor the enmity of Satan. In Christ their eternal life is **secure**. Their only fear should be lest they surrender the truth, and thus betray the trust with which God has honored them.[1]

As long as you are true to yourself, no adverse power of earth or hell will be able to destroy your peace or interrupt your communion with God. If you fear God, you need not walk in **uncertainty**.[2]

If we fear God we need fear nothing else!

♦ Further discussion on the relationship between the fear of God and assurance may be found in Chapter 3 under "Assurance of a God Who Listens," and in Chapter 7 under "Assurance of Safety (Security)."

11. ASSURANCE AND ABIDING IN JESUS

Hereby we know that he abideth in us, by the Spirit which he hath given us.[3]

In Chapter 2 under the topic, "Assurance of an Intimately Present, Abiding Christ," there has been discussion of this heart-warming subject. Included below is a gem on assurance which did not seem as appropriate there.

["The soul that is imbued with the love of Jesus"] loves to contemplate Jesus, and by beholding him, will become changed into his likeness. Christ is formed within, the hope of glory [Colossians 1:27]. His **confidence** increases that he is loved of God, and his love deepens and widens, as he has the **assurance** that he is abiding in Christ and Christ in him [John 15:4].[4]

---

[1] *The Desire of Ages,* 356.

[2] *This Day with God,* 334 (Letter 11-21-1879, to Edson).

[3] 1 John 3:24.

[4] *The Youth's Instructor,* 8-9-1894, ¶ 7.

12. ASSURANCE AND WITNESSING

There is one great principle of the law of God, out of which all other laws flow—the principle of love. This over-arching principle has two branches, love for God and love for our fellow human beings.[1] From these two branches spring all the valid laws that prescribe the behavior of every creature in the universe. We seek the happiness of those we love, and mind and heart are ever active in arranging opportunities so that we may be close to them.

Similarly, God's love for us is stronger than death, and so He seeks both our happiness and to be close to us. The behavior of God's children, who inherit His character, is therefore also characterized by love for Him and for His other children, as well as for those who are only eligible to *become* His children. Different consequences of this line of thought are pursued in Chapter 2 under the topic, "Assurance of an Intimately Present, Abiding Christ," and in Chapter 7 under "Assurance of Happiness."

Continuing the above line of reasoning—that, if we are God's children, we have a great desire for the happiness of others and to be close to them—we are led to a most effective way of witnessing through our love for our fellowmen, including lost sinners. We seek their happiness by introducing them to the most delightful experience human beings can have, *viz.,* an understanding of the love experience it is their privilege to have with God. This cascade of witnessing continues as we open to them the delights of realizing such an experience with God by being *ourselves* "loving and lovable" Christians.[2] We thus become flesh-and-

---

[1] Luke 10:26-28.

[2] "[Christ's] words bore with them a convincing power because they came from a heart pure and holy, full of love and sympathy, benevolence and truth.... The strongest argument in favor of the gospel is *a loving and lovable Christian*." —*The Ministry of Healing,* 469f. Observable results of being a "loving and lovable Christian" are described as follows: "Kind words, pleasant looks, a cheerful countenance throw a

blood, living witnesses to the exhilarating joy available to the sinner through his living in the warm, inviting atmosphere of God's love that begins with the inclusive, satisfying love relationship he has with those who are God's witnesses.

It is evident that the above discussion involves a luxuriance of feeling. In this light it is quite important that it is not feeling that is calling the shots, defining the rules of behavior, or deciding the genuineness of the experience. The Word of God does all that. As we immerse ourselves in God's love letters to us we will have strong feelings about God and others that are *consequences* of a relationship with God which is defined by His word.

> How can we possibly lead others to a full **assurance**, to simple, childlike faith in our heavenly Father, when we are measuring and judging our love to him by our feelings?[1]

This affirms that to bring others to a satisfying, enduring love experience with God we must ourselves have more than a superficial love relationship with Him—more than a shallow affinity that is analogous to an infatuation between two human beings based only on physical *feeling*, arising from within, rather than a deep, lasting love arising from above. This latter experience is by no means feelingless, but it is *much more* than feeling,[2] and is something out of which strong feelings grow, and without which effective witnessing cannot exist. I repeat here a powerful comment which describes a most important condition for effective witnessing.

> [T]he divine **assurance** which [Jesus' disciples, after Pentecost] manifested was an evidence to men that they had received the gift of the Holy Ghost. *Men's hearts were*

charm around the Christian that makes his influence almost irresistible." —*Review and Herald*, 9-1-1885, ¶ 3. Also in *Signs of the Times*, 9-8-1890. ¶ 3. in a different context.

[1] *Signs of the Times*, 12-3-1894. ¶ 7.

[2] See the topic. "Assurance and Feeling." earlier in this chapter.

melted and subdued. The promise, "Greater works than these shall he do" [John 14:12], was fulfilled.[1]

It is neither sugary *words* nor sound *theories,* but attractive, loving *lives* that make us effective witnesses. We certainly do not wish to be found promoting *unsound* theories, but it is practical godliness that we need.

> Through our *lives* the despondent may receive an **assurance** that it is possible to be partakers of the divine nature, and by taking hold of this divinity win the victory that all must win who shall enter in through the gates into the city.[2]

♦ For further discussion on the relationship between assurance and the divine nature see the topic, "Assurance That We May Receive the Divine Nature," in chapter 7.

> The words are addressed to you, "Let *your*[3] light so shine before men, that they may see your good works, and glorify your father which is in heaven" [Matthew 5:16]. The words in favor of truth spoken with the **assurance** that comes from the possession of a right purpose, and in cheerful hope, from a pure heart, will make the angels rejoice.[4]

We are surrounded by a world filled with fearful, anxious people. Therefore our words, to be effective in witnessing to the truth, must be able to create assurance in the minds of men where there was none! This can be done only by grace Thus we have God's delightful promise that He "fills our lips with assurance."[5]

The adjective "tame" occurs scores of times in the inspired writings in connection with witnessing, always in an unfavorable light. This is in connection with the fact that no tame, spiritless presentation of

---

[1] *Review and Herald,* 6-18-1895, ¶ 7. Emphases added.

[2] *Sermons and Talks,* II, 294 (3-10-1908). Emphases added.

[3] Italic in the original.

[4] *Sons and Daughters of God,* 276 (1908).

[5] *Testimonies for the Church,* VII, 71.

truth can be effective in outreach, in leading others to assurance of salvation. We can make room for only two of these.

> The Word of God must be administered with spirit and with life.... A tame, uncertain delivery will do no good.... We can have the most precious truths, and deliver them in such a tame, uncertain, lifeless manner in the interpretation, as to crush out from the precious meaning all the power to impress hearts and awaken consciousness.[1]

> The warfare is before us. No tame message will have influence now.[2]

Since a "tame message" will have no beneficial influence, I conclude this section with what kind of a message *will* have the needed influence.

> One who would be a teacher of sacred things should not go forth to work with the people without a full **assurance** that he has the truth.... Anything short of a full **conviction** that what he presents is truth will make his preaching powerless.[3]

> There are ... many to receive the joy of salvation into their own souls.... God has joy to restore to them, even the joy of His anointed. This will give efficiency and happiness and sanctified **assurance**—a living testimony.[4]

13. PERFECT ASSURANCE

> In Christ the guilty heart has found relief. He is the sure foundation. All who make Him their dependence rest in **perfect security**.[5]

---

[1] *Manuscript Releases*, X, 134 (1896).

[2] *Temperance*, 239 (1897).

[3] *EGW 1888 Materials*, 170 (Minneapolis, 11-1-1888).

[4] *The Upward Look*, 287 (1896).

[5] *The Desire of Ages*, 599.

Doubt, unbelief, prejudice, and stubbornness, killed all love from their [rejecters of 1888 message] souls. They demanded *perfect* **assurance**, but this is not compatible with faith.[1]

"Then looking unto Jesus, who is the author and finisher of our faith [Hebrews 12:2], with **perfect assurance** we may commit the keeping our souls unto him, *while we cooperate with divine agencies*.[2]

Though multitudes are pressing on in the wrong way, though the outlook be ever so discouraging, yet we may have *full* **assurance** in our Leader; for 'I am God,' he declares, 'and there is none else' [Isaiah 45:22; 46:9, &c].[3]

◆ Compare the above section with the sections, "Assurance and Maturity," in this chapter; " and with "Assurance of Growth," in Chapter 5.

14. UNJUSTIFIED ASSURANCE

We discussed briefly in the Introduction within the setting of the contest between David and the Philistine giant, Goliath, that there are assurances of happy outcomes in trying situations that are the result of seemingly sound reasoning (using all the evidence one has) from a human point of view, but which are nevertheless proved eventually to be completely unjustified. Goliath's failure to survive the encounter with David provides a proof in the specific context of 1 Samuel 17. Much of what is currently termed "assurance" is of just such a character, a structure of human fabrication that works fine for a time, as it did for Goliath, and then fails you in the end.

As also pointed out in the Introduction, such a man-made philosophy of assurance also worked temporarily for Simon

---

[1] *EGW 1888 Materials,* 1029 (To General Conference President, O. A. Olsen, concerning those who rejected the message of righteousness by faith at the 1888 General Conference).

[2] *Signs of the Times,* 1-15-93, ¶ 8. Italic added.

[3] *Review and Herald,* 6-9-1910, ¶ 9.

Peter, Saul of Tarsus, and for many others down to the present time, including perhaps some readers of this book. It will never do, however, for us to come up to the trials of the last days (*we're there!*) with no firmer footing than had these men of the less seductive times of the past. When all the froth is blown away it becomes apparent that the real difference between the assurance of David and the assurance of Goliath boils down to the difference between faith and presumption.

> Many who claim to be sanctified, who are yet breaking the commandments of God, and filled with enmity against God, are boldly presumptuous, and while disobeying the words of Christ, yet dare to appropriate the promises given to the loyal and obedient.... But their *presumptuous* **assurance** is not faith. They do not know what constitutes faith.[1]

The difference between exercising faith and presumption, on my part, is simple but subtle. Presumption is an assumption which under some given set of conditions is unjustified, but which under some non-identical set of conditions is entirely appropriate. The difference between the two sets of conditions is that in the latter (the case of faith), one condition over-arches all the others, *viz.,* one has determined (decided, chosen, willed) that *God shall direct his steps—all* of them.[2] In the former, some*one* or some*thing* else is participating in giving him direction.

In the Bible God has spoken to us personally His directions for our "steps," and interpreted these directions by His Spirit who has given us a score of millions of words explaining the biblical instructions so that none who can read need be misdirected. For those who have no access to the written word, He has made understandable the Omnipotent's "eternal power and Godhead" "by the things that are made," so that

---

[1] *Signs of the Times,* 2-28-1895. ¶ 7.

[2] See Proverbs 3:5. 6.

through the natural world, "the invisible things of [God] from the creation of the world are clearly ... understood."[1] For Further discussion of God's personal help in understanding His directions, see the topic, "Assurance That God's Word Is True," in Chapter 6.

> We are not to rest **quietly**, with the thought that the devil will have nothing to do with us; but we can have the **assurance** that we shall not be left helpless, to be overcome by him.[2]

If this is my situation, my presumption is that, if I "rest quietly," that is, do nothing, then Satan will leave me alone.

> To the young ruler [Matthew 19] who declared that he had kept the commandments from his youth up, and with *self-assurance* asked, "What lack I yet?" Christ said, "If thou wilt be perfect, go and sell that thou hast, and give to the poor, and thou shalt have treasure in heaven; and come and follow Me" [Matthew 19:20, 21].... His lack was plainly revealed.[3]

This young man walked away with nothing but unjustified assurance because, although he asked for and was willing to receive some direction from Jesus, self, money, and power were playing a role in directing his steps. Furthermore this man was obliquely making a statement about his own supposed "goodness" when he called Jesus "good"; was he not also a "master"? The statement that follows affirms that any such feelings of goodness can leave us with only unjustified assurance.

> There are efforts made in our own strength, but there is not a dying to self, the soul is not surrendered to God. Many are making a mistake here. They are hoping to overcome through their own efforts, and *by their goodness* gain the

---

[1] Romans 1:20.

[2] *Review and Herald,* 7-9-1908, ¶ 13 (Sermon, 3-7-1908).

[3] *Signs of the Times,* 7-21-1898, ¶ 12. Emphases added.

assurance of the love of God. They do not exercise faith; they do not believe that Jesus accepts their repentance and contrition, and so they toil on day after day without finding rest or peace.[1]

Ultimately, unjustified assurance is based upon confidence in what created beings can do with the beings and things which God has created. The ultimate basis for justified assurance is confidence in what the Creator can do with the beings and things which He creates. The former has limited power, knowledge, and presence. The latter has unlimited power, knowledge, and presence—often designated by the terms omnipotence, omniscience, and omnipresence, respectively. These distinctions, together with the fact that "God is love," make clear why assurance based on the former will ultimately disappoint us, whereas we can never be disappointed by assurance based on the latter. Furthermore, justified assurance can be had by all, because such things as human sources of talent, money, power, family, friends, and position play no part!

15. THE RAINBOW OF ASSURANCE

These final thoughts upon which the book ends should direct our vision heavenward.

> As we gaze upon the beautiful sight [a rainbow], we may be joyful in God, **assured** that he himself is looking upon this token of his covenant, and that as he looks upon it he remembers the children of earth, to whom it was given.[2]

> The rainbow round about the throne is an **assurance** that God is true, that in Him is no variableness, neither shadow of turning [James 1:17].[3]

---

[1] *Review and Herald*, 5-20-1884, ¶ 6 (Morning talk to ministers, 1883 General Conference). Emphases added.

[2] *Ibid.*, 2-26-1880, ¶ 7.

[3] *Christ's Object Lessons*, 148.

"These things are to be often in mind. Meditate upon them…. '[G]ive diligence to make your calling and election **sure.**' 2 Peter 1:10. We need not have a *supposed* hope, but an **assurance**."[1]

The author allows the delightful anticipation of soon being a neighbor in the New Jerusalem of the readers of this book.

---

[1] *Manuscript Releases,* XIX, 351 (Ms 13, 1884). (The last two sentences are also in *Our High Calling,* 74.)